samirCinema
The Journal of Modern Film, Television & Streaming

Vol. 1

Edited by Amir Said and Amir Ali Said
Created by Amir Said

New York

Samir Cinema
Volume 1
Published by Superchamp Books

Copyright © 2020 Superchamp Books, Inc.

A Superchamp Books First Paperback Edition

All Rights Reserved.
No part of this book may be reproduced in any form by any electronic or mechanical means, including information storage and retrieval systems, without the expressed written permission of the publisher, except by a reviewer, who may quote brief passages in a review. Published by Superchamp Books, Inc. www.superchampbooks.com.

Superchamp Books™ is a trademark of Superchamp, Inc.

Editor, Amir Ali Said
Series Creator and Editor, Amir Said

DESIGNED BY AMIR SAID

Cover, Design, and Layout by Amir Said

Print History:
November 2020: First printing.

Samir Cinema: Volume 1
/ Edited by Amir Ali Said
Series Editor Amir Said
1. Said, Amir Ali 2. Said, Amir 3. Film Criticism 4. Movie Criticism
5. Television Criticism
I. Said, Amir Ali; Said, Amir II. Title

ISBN 978-1-64404-000-3 (Paperback)

CONTENTS

INTRODUCTION   1

Could Alex Garland Be Reshaping The Landscape For Female Representation In Science Fiction?
   Haaniyah Angus   5

How *The Truman Show* Warned Us About Social Media (Before It Was Invented)
   Tom Trott   11

There Is No Spoon
   Eric Pierce   17

The Screams Of Women In Film And What *Twin Peaks* Can Teach Us About It
   Ariana DiValentino   23

Coraline and Freud. Distinguishing Being and Semblance
   Timofei Gerber   33

Review: *Touch Of Evil*
   Julien Allen   43

Get Out and The Revolutionary Act of Subverting The White Gaze
   Dianca London   49

How Documentary Film Became Entertainment
   Josh Rose   57

This Magnificent Cake Pokes Fun At Black People and Gets The Belgian Congo All Wrong
   Jumko Ogata   69

Break Up the Media Giants
   Paris Marx   77

TCM Diary: Jane Fonda In the 1960s
   Beatrice Loayza   89

All Steadicam and No Play: Movement in The Shining
Anya Stanley   95

Black Panther Raises Big Questions about Identity and Loyalty
Doc Ayomide   103

The Beautiful Girls: The Dynamic Women of *Mad Men*
Angela Morrison   111

Everything Daniel Kaluuya Revealed On The Set of *Queen & Slim*
Jerry Barrow   119

Interpreting the Ending of *Crouching Tiger Hidden Dragon*
Stephen Cobbe   125

Waves: An Anti-Black Coming of Age Film
Fatima Ali Omar   137

Miyazaki's Beautiful Antiwar Dreams
Dan Sanchez   143

Going to The Beginning - The Art of Screenwriting: 1910s
Seraphima Bogomolova   159

How the Symmetry and Aesthetics of The Handmaid's Tale Is Essential to Its Storytelling
Zofia Wijaszka   169

The Brilliance of Zack Snyder's DC Universe
Christopher Pierznik   175

Why Ava DuVernay's When They See Us Is The Torturous Masterclass In Systemic Assault
Ezinne Ukoha   201

"Stay away from the door!": The Women of John Carpenter's The Fog
Sydney Urbanek   209

'We Are Too Rare': The Importance of Inclusivity Behind Spike Lee's *She's Gotta Have It* Reboot
Katie Tandy   217

Into the Vortex: *Vertigo* (1958)
  Lary Wallace   229

CREDITS   239

ACKNOWLEDGMENTS   243

INTRODUCTION

The Importance of Film Education

Film, like music, is deeply embedded into our personal and collective existence. Film adds depth and dimension to our environment, it elevates the human spirit, and it contributes in many important ways to our quality of life. Moreover, film is one of the primary ways that we learn about ourselves and others. Film is also crucial to our understanding of the different traditions and beliefs that exist around the world. Film is also one of the fundamental ways that we create and communicate in and draw meaning from the world around us. This is why everyone — regardless of age, cultural heritage, or socio-economic background — benefits from a diverse film education.

Thus, the purpose of film education, and by proxy film journals and other film education books like *Samir Cinema*, is not only to inform but to enrich and enlighten us all. With film education books, people increase their awareness of rich and diverse cultures, beliefs, and societies; and they learn how and why almost nothing in contemporary society is created or communicated without the influence of film.

Academic Journals, Book Anthologies, and *Samir Cinema*

There is a lot of good writing happening today. From the explosion of talented essayists to freelance writers to independent authors to DIY poets and more, this era is rapidly producing some of the most engaging and culturally influential writing ever published. At the same time, however, much of this writing is being missed by the very readers who would likely appreciate and benefit from it the most. This is not to say that a lot of the great writing of today is being overlooked, but rather that the number of literary channels — and their outdated publishing methods and often non-inclusive traditions — is insufficient to the growing body of interesting writing that's taking place right now. And this is especially the case when it comes to academic journals and contemporary book anthologies.

Academic journals and book anthologies are a great way to discover new writers and a means for further understanding the art and craft of writing. For classic Western literature, the task of assembling an academic journal or an anthology tends to be a foregone conclusion, at least in terms of who should have the privilege to be published. But I don't believe that academic journals, which are typically walled-off to the general public, and contemporary book anthologies need to suffer from a similar ideological, non-inclusive fate.

More specifically, the inclusive kind of academic journals and book anthologies — that I believe better serve new voices in writing — do not exist in tall order. Academic journals and book anthologies, which have typically been fashioned by a narrow group of people whose tastes are tuned to an even more narrow corner of writing, are often positioned well outside of the mainstream and general public. Because of this, I believe the potential of the academic journal and book anthology, as a combined form and as a pop culture item, is largely unrecognized. That's why I created *Samir Cinema*. I want to help academic journals and anthologies become a more recognizable part of mainstream and pop culture, not something merely for scholars or so-called literary types. Moreover, I want to reimagine what the academic journal and book anthology is; how it's shaped, who it's for, and how it works.

I think academic journals and book anthologies are like music playlists for readers, but loads of informationn and insight. And just like music playlists, literary playlists benefit from the specific tastes and backgrounds of its curators. Within this context I believe that there is a premium for curated literature that stands beyond bloated listicles or selection archetypes commonly found among literary elitists. Amir, the co-editor of *Samir Cinema*, and I have cultivated our tastes from a broad consumption of literature, music, film, art, and pop culture. Certainly, this is not to say that our tastes are superior to anyone else's, but rather it's fine tuned to the areas of culture that we've long had deep interest in and, in many cases, that we have written or read extensively about. In this light, Amir and I want *Samir Cinema* to be an academic journal and book anthology that promotes some of the finest writing in film.

As to what constitutes the "finest" writing within this area, well, I base this not so much on my (or Amir's) personal tastes but on what I believe are the three things that academic journals and book anthologies should do. First, I believe that an academic journal and book anthology should be about discovery. It should introduce writers to new audiences; conversely, it should introduce audiences to emerging and established writers whose work deserves further amplification. Second, I believe that an academic journal and book anthology should offer insight into the craft of writing. That is to say, it should offer a close-up on style and form and the different ways in which themes are developed by writers. Finally, I believe that an academic journal and book anthology should always offer fresh perspectives and insights to the field that it expolres. The kind of perspective and insights that illuminate current cultural moments and shed light on important points from the past.

Amir Said,
Creator and Editor-In-Chief, *Samir Cinema*

Could Alex Garland Be Reshaping The Landscape For Female Representation In Science Fiction?

by Haaniyah Angus[1]

It seems that author turned filmmaker Alex Garland has set his sights among the genre of Science Fiction. With *Ex Machina* (2014) and *Annihilation* (2018) under his belt, it would not be too early to say that the director has made a name for himself by reexamining old tropes within the genre when it comes to gender representation. Both his films *Ex Machina* and *Annihilation* feature women as leads, with *Annihilation* bringing in five female characters. The two centre around differing Science Fiction topics, *Ex Machina* deals with AI and technological innovations, while *Annihilation* examines extraterrestrial life forms.

The discourse surrounding gender representation in Science Fiction (SF) has existed since its Golden Age and beyond. Golden Age SF was almost exclusively written by men, purchased by men or boys; and its conventions were shaped by the passions and interests of adolescent males. Even though the undisputed founder of SF to many is Mary Shelley, women within the genre were pushed out of it altogether. It would seem that women were not reflected within the audiences that consumed SF but on the contrary, they read it and wrote about it, they just didn't get published as writers nor critics.

Even Isaac Asimov, who's shaped our conception of robotics and AI like few others, thought that "swooning dames" had no place in sci-fi, and after being rebuked in a readers' letter by a Ms.

---

[1] Haaniyah Angus is a third-year Media and Communications student at Oxford Brookes University. She is also an internet culture critic as well as a screenwriter.

Mary Rogers[2], declared "that women never affected the world directly, they always grabbed hold of some poor, innocent man, worked their insidious wiles on him and then affected history through him." As good an indicator as any to what exact world female SF fans and creatives were venturing into. For many, they were marginalised by a genre that celebrated exploring new worlds and progressive ideals. Garland directly opposes this not only by placing women at the forefront of his stories but actively attempting to disband old tropes used against them.

Ex Machina places Alicia Vikander as a female AI (artificial intelligence) known as Ava, created by tech billionaire Nathan (Oscar Isaac). In the film Nathan invites Caleb (Domhnall Gleeson), a young programmer, to participate in what is known as a 'Turing Test' wherein which AI is tested against human intelligence to see if its reasonings are indistinguishable from a human mind's. Through the different tests, Caleb falls in love with Ava, and she uses his weakness against him to help her escape and rid her of her master.

The reception of *Ex Machina*'s use of a female AI was not overwhelmingly positive: for some Ava is a modern day retelling of past female AI tropes from films such as *Metropolis* (1927). Argued by Angela Watercutter for *WIRED*[3]: 'she uses her sexuality to get what she wants, and the camera frames her as an object of desire. (…) Ava is the smartest creature on screen at all times, but the message we are left with at the end of *Ex Machina* is still that the best way for a miraculously intelligent creature to get what she wants is to flirt manipulatively.'

However, this criticism ignores the fundamental change of pace with Garland's work. Garland is not framing Ava this way in order to undermine her as a remarkable creation but instead

---

[2] Rogers, Evelyn, Mary, II, Rogers, Michael, James, "Letter," (2006), "Astounding Science Fiction," September 1939, p. 97 http://justinelarbalestier.com/books/battle/letters/

[3] Watercutter, A., "Ex Machina Has a Serious Fembot Problem, WIRED (April 9, 2015) https://www.wired.com/2015/04/ex-machina-turing-bechdel-test/

to give the viewer Caleb's POV (point of view). She is sexualised because he instantly is attracted to her and, realising that in order to manipulate Caleb into helping her escape Nathan she must use sex as a weapon, she turns his attraction against him. Ava never uses her sexuality for anything other than self-preservation, and it makes sense as to why she would do so. Ava is stuck within the confines of a house where, if she does not live up to the standards of Nathan, he would most likely turn her into a sex robot.

Ex Machina is an explicit critique of both 'Nerdy Misogyny' (Nathan) and 'White Knights' (Caleb). Nathan is what many would call a 'tech bro', a male who typically works in a field devoid of women and thus does not know how to converse with them and does not treat them as human. While Caleb may also fall into that category, unlike Nathan, he is looking for companionship but only on his terms. He fetishises Ava and creates a fantasy of her in his head, one in which he saves her from Nathan. Garland could have not sexualised Ava or had her not flirt with Caleb, but that ultimately would have changed the core message behind the movie. Seeking to redress the imbalance by producing more positive representations of women is futile if the underlying material conditions went unreformed; in other words, negative images may be accurate. The reason as to why this film helps change the long-standing harmful tropes towards female AI is that Ava wins at the end, she gets to escape and enact revenge on the men who infantilised her and sexualised her. She is aware of the games that they are playing with her and so plays along to get what she wanted all along. Ava is not the damsel in distress but instead the mastermind.

However, while *Ex Machina* did deconstruct SF tropes, the film starred two female characters with only Ava in a speaking role. With only 30.2% of the 30,835 speaking characters between 2007 and 2014 being female across the 700 top-grossing films (Smith et al. 2015), *Ex Machina* does lack representation in not only the number of female characters but also in regards to race and sexuality. With regards to race, especially, Asian[4] critics have written about the particular kind of dehumanization that Kyoko[5] (Sonoya Mizuno) suffers in order to further the liberation of an AI who, if nothing else, looks like a white woman. One may argue that Garland's follow up to *Ex Machina* improves upon *Ex Machina's* demographic, with a leading cast composed of five women, two of them being women of colour. Though *Annihilation* takes a significant step back by whitewashing[6] the two most significant female roles: in the original book, the biologist was said to have Asian heritage, while the psychologist was described as Native American.

Garland's adaptation of the 2014 novel *Annihilation* centres around five female scientists who embark on a journey to enter 'The Shimmer', an unknown quarantined zone full of mutating organic lifeforms. The team consists of Lena (Natalie Portman), Dr Ventress (Jennifer Jason Leigh), Josie (Tessa Thompson), Anya (Gina Rodriguez) and Cass (Tuva Novotny). In comparison to SF of the 1950s, where misogynist 'lady land' films such as *Cat-Women of the Moon* (1953) and *Fire Maidens from Outer Space* (1956) would depict faraway lands that exist solely in order to be discovered and colonised by lucky male astronauts, a film such as *Annihilation* is worlds away in terms of representation. Not only do we get a female-led ensemble but there are characters who are Black and

---

[4] Kim, Jeremiah, "Extra Ex Machina: asian bodies as disposable, alien(ated) labor in American sci-fi," Kitsch (December 26, 2017)
https://kitschcornell.com/2017/12/26/extra-ex-machina-asian-bodies-as-disposable-alienated-labor-in-american-sci-fi/

[5] Chang, H, Sharon, "How 'Ex Machina' Abuses Women of Color & Nobody Cares Cause It's Smart," Multiracial Asian Families (May 30, 2015)
https://multiasianfamilies.blogspot.com/2015/05/how-ex-machina-abuses-women-of-color.html

[6] Dong, Kelley, ""Annihilation" and Alex Garland's Wrestlings With Asian Bodies," Village Voice (March 16, 2018)
https://www.villagevoice.com/2018/03/16/annihilation-and-alex-garlands-wrestlings-with-asian-american-bodies/

Latinx (overlapping with Thompson), as well as a lesbian character, both of which are rarely seen within SF but are becoming more and more frequent in contemporary fiction.

The freedom of choice granted to these characters is hardly ever found in SF. Women across media and particularly in this male-dominated genre are often made to choose between binaries set before them, such as scientist/woman, mind/body, subject/object, culture/nature and self/other. Historically in SF, female scientists struggle to be perceived in relation to the first terms, while in comparison male characters and the films themselves align her with the second.

Annihilation does not attempt to put its female characters within a box, police them or hide their flaws. The film allows them to be emotionally vulnerable but still full of agency, something not seen often in SF. Ventress has the most power and authority, and due to her circumstance, has seen so many teams of hers fail, that she has grown distant and apathetic, which is traditionally a characterization that falls in line with more 'lone wolf' male archetypes. After her death, Lena is the one who ends the journey taken at the start of the film, her husband Kane (Oscar Isaac) is her driving force (a role often assigned to dead or endangered girlfriends, wives or, sometimes, daughters), but he does not make up her entire character. The story starts and ends with her, no saviour necessary, no need to push the idea that she can not do it alone.

However, some may suggest that even with the leaps and bounds of female representation within SF due to Garland, that he ultimately does not understand the experiences of women and thus his depictions will never be genuinely tailored to them nor would it be free of any implicit gender biases he may hold. For many, Garland could be seen as either someone pushing female representation in SF forward or someone taking up well-deserved space that a female creative could hold; and maybe even both.

This may be due to how the 'image of woman' has been a site of gendered discourse, drawn from the specific sociocultural experiences of women and shared by women, which negotiates a space within, and sometimes resists patriarchal domination. In other words, can a man genuinely create depictions of women that propel them forward?

Denial of female subjectivity recurs throughout SF because of the social relations of filmmaking are, like those of science, 'highly integrated with' and tend to reproduce 'the larger social relations of the societies that support them'. While there is not an inherent issue with male creatives writing or directing female-driven stories in SF, it may be more helpful to use female perspectives. Working with female writers, directors, cinematographers, editors and other female creatives will make sure that checks and balances are in place for male creatives. It would also help with ensuring that the representation is authentic and three dimensional instead of a quick cash grab from filmgoers.

You cannot please all audiences with your representation but the attempt to right the wrongs of an industry that historically has hidden women from SF is far from the wrong choice. Garland is only two films deep into his budding directorial career but it seems that the direction he is heading towards is attempting to open the gates long held shut for women in Science Fiction.

How *The Truman Show* Warned Us About Social Media (Before It Was Invented)

by Tom Trott[7]

The Truman Show (1998) is perhaps one of the most interpretable films ever made. In just 103-minutes it presents and teases apart a wide range of themes: our relationship with television and media, the way large companies control and curate our lives through representation, the way we filter real life through the narrative structures of popular storytelling, and many more.

In the mix is a theme often neglected when discussing the *The Truman Show* because, unlike the ones listed above, the film doesn't examine it through the fictional audience's experience of watching "The Truman Show", but instead through Truman Burbank's experience of it. It's a theme that seemed less important in the late-1990s, but one that has risen in relevance in our Instagram-filtered world: the public vs. private self.

The Truman Show (directed by Peter Weir, written by Andrew Niccol) follows Truman Burbank's (Jim Carrey) slow realisation that his life is, and always has been, broadcast live around the world for people's entertainment. His hometown of Seahaven is nothing but a huge set, and its residents, including his wife and best friend, are all actors playing their part.

Television is all-consuming in the world of *The Truman Show*, and social media doesn't exist. This is because the film was released

---

[7] Tom Trott is a film journalist and author from Brighton, UK. He has a first-class honours degree in Film Studies from the University of Sussex, won the Empire Award (thriller category) in the 2015 New York Screenplay Contest, and has written four novels. He writes for framerated.co.uk and feature articles can be found on Medium at medium.com/@tomtrott

20 years ago, before the invention of Facebook, Twitter, Instagram, or even MySpace. Before we would start broadcasting our lives by choice rather than deception.

But despite it predating social media, viewing the film from a 2018 perspective lends it even deeper layers of meaning. If one imagines Truman's town of Seahaven as an online space, we see that by examining the public v. private self, the film warned us about three particularly modern dangers.

Catfish

It's the actors in Truman's life that most obviously represent the dissonance between the public and private self. In the world of the film, Louis Coltrane (Noah Emmerich) plays Marlon, Truman's best friend since childhood. He's the person Truman confides in most closely and shares his hopes and fears with. But the Marlon he thinks he knows doesn't exist. As demonstrated painfully when Christof (Ed Harris), the creator, producer, and director of "The Truman Show", feeds Louis (as Marlon) the line:

"The last thing I would ever do is lie to you."

Truman's been "catfished" by everyone in his life; tricked into relationships by people presenting false personas. This has been achieved in the most classical fashion by Truman's wife Meryl (actually an actor named Hannah Gill, played by Laura Linney).

Meryl/Hannah didn't really fall in love with Truman, she was just playing a part, as represented comically when Truman notices she crossed her fingers in their wedding photo. Ultimately she was doing it for money, or whatever else she gains from being on "The Truman Show".

In 1998, this was unique to the world of *The Truman Show*, and those unfortunate enough to be fooled in a romance or friendship scam. In 2018's online world, it is so common we have a new word, a documentary, and television series about it.

Everyone in Truman's life has a public persona as curated and false as the average Instagram feed, but the similarities don't end there: both Marlon and Meryl push products that they pretend to enjoy at the behest of the producers. They become living, breathing adverts for products.

In 1998 this was a joke about product placement (and still is), but in 2018 this behaviour is indistinguishable from that of a social media influencer. People paid by companies to use their products and share positive posts and videos about them. Living, breathing adverts, using their audience's affection and trust to profit from their performed authenticity.

Marlon and Meryl are not only catfish, but also influencers: Meryl extolling the wonders of kitchen utensils and hot chocolate drinks; Marlon of beer.

However, in this case Truman isn't the intended audience, the audience watching "The Truman Show" are. With social media influencers this distinction isn't as clear. We aren't just their audience, we are their "friends" and "followers", encouraged to connect with them. It's as if the Marlons and Meryls of our lives were pushing those products on us, Truman, not the audience.

Hannah's, Louis's, and other influencer's real feelings are irrelevant because their public and private selves are separate (they're just actors), even as that distinction is deliberately blurred. Many of us are now aware of that, but still it is just as painful to discover we have been lied to.

Profiling

The third malevolent element of social media that *The Truman Show* warned us about was profiling, achieved in the digital age through constant surveillance and the retention and analysis of data.

Truman is watched and recorded everywhere he goes, and this is used to build up information about his patterns and behaviour, which are then used to provide him with a version of things he wants. But this is only a way to keep him content in Seahaven, not to truly make him happy. The producers give him Meryl, when really he wants Lauren (really Sylvia, played by Natasha McElhone). They give him the return of his father, when really he wants to escape.

This is no different to how digital companies give us another post/video/feature to keep us satisfied but still inside the system, when what we really want is to turn off our phone or delete our account completely. It's nothing but temporary placation to distract from underlying unease. In 2018, we've all become Truman, contained in our digital Seahaven.

By presenting a false world, designed to give the illusion of genuine human connection, but really designed to make a profit for those in charge, *The Truman Show* warned us about the dangers of social media before it was even invented. So what does the film say we should do about these malevolent forces?

Escape

At the end of the film, as Truman is on the verge of leaving, Christof offers him a deal: stay in the safe world of Seahaven where he will be a star and he will always be content, and in return all he will have to consent to is being watched every moment of his life. These are Christof's terms and conditions, if you will.

He tells Truman that he already knows he will accept them because he knows him better than anyone else. Why does he make this claim? Because he has been watching him his entire life. Profiling him. To which Truman replies,

"You never had a camera in my head."

The same way we reject Facebook's claims to understand our emotions when it chooses to remind us of a tragic event from seven years ago; Google's claims to understand our interests when it recommends a restaurant we have already tried and hated; and Amazon's claims to understand what we want left in our neighbours' bin.

And this is because Truman also has a private self that is distinct from his public self. Like us all he presents one version of himself through his social interaction, in his case a carefully performed cheerfulness, whilst masking his private self, in his case a pervading unhappiness. This is perhaps the element of real-world social interaction that has been most magnified by transferring it online.

Separation of the public and private self is not just something that is done to us by catfish and influencers, it is also something we, like Truman, do ourselves. Just as my profile here on Medium describes me as an independent author (which I am) but ignores the other job I do to pay my rent.

Ignorance

But there is a key difference between Truman and us: Truman didn't know he was being filmed, didn't know his friends and family were lying, didn't know his entire world was built and controlled by powerful men whose interests may start as altruistic or simply naive, but are ultimately egotistical.

But we know.

Unlike Truman, we've chosen to broadcast our lives. There's a cynical part of me that wonders if most of us wouldn't be thrilled to discover we were the star of our own reality TV show. Keeping Up With the Burbanks.

Unlike Truman we've heard Christof's offer and accepted it. We've become adept at presenting a public self that is distinct from our private self, and yet many of us still fail to recognise that distinction in others.

> We still get fooled, betrayed, and hurt online.
> The Truman Show tried to warn us 20 years ago.
> We didn't listen.

There Is No Spoon
by Eric Pierce[8]

The Matrix is a seminal piece of film-making, ground-breaking and stylistic and just plain cool. But lately, I tend not to gravitate to the slick action sequences or the chic goth aesthetic or even the mind-bending ramifications of a computer simulation so real it is imperceptible from the real thing.

Remember the scene at the office where Neo works? We linger just long enough to get the gist: cubicle farms and soul-sucking fluorescent lights and programming that is rather meaningless in the scheme of things.

It is a familiar place.

Neo is given a chance to escape this hapless place, but once out on the ledge, his resolve quickly melts. It's too risky. He goes back inside, resigned to whatever awaits.

The movie's central question— "What is the Matrix?"— could just as easily be interpreted as "What is Life?"

During high school, I worked part-time bagging groceries. It was a small town, and the store was one of the few businesses that employed more than fifty people, which meant my co-workers were that curious stew of young and old, hopeful and resigned, all temporarily bound together by fate and the never-ending quest for money.

I worked with friends from school; twenty-somethings who saw the job as a pit stop on the way to elsewhere; the middle-aged whom had been twenty, once, but were now held hostage by mortgages and kids; grizzled sixty year-olds running out the clock.

---

[8] Eric Pierce is the author of Clockwork Scoundrels, which is a love letter to the television show Firefly. He writes frequently on Medium and is editor of the pop culture publication FanFare. Eric lives in Michigan and is probably thinking about Star Wars.

There was tension between the older employees and high schoolers. Born partly of the natural jealousy the old harbor the young for their effortless vitality, partly because kids can be stupidly immature, and partly from knowing we were bound to other, different fates, ones they felt were intrinsically better than theirs. Trapped by circumstance, bad luck, or poor choices, they were doomed to remain forever behind, forgotten.

We Were A Reminder Of What Could've Been, And They Hated Us For It.

Rex was different. For one, he smiled, unabashedly indifferent to his handful of missing teeth. He was also the only bagger older than twenty, a stocky fifty year-old with closely cropped gray hair and the round gut of a life-long drinker. He rode a rusty old bicycle, rain or shine or snow, and he freely dispensed wisdom like he'd a right to it, a Caucasian Buddha in an apron holding court to indifferent teenagers.

He was the sort of person it's almost impossible to dislike, seemingly unflappable to the winds of fate, quick to share a laugh or a ribald joke.

Looking back, I can't help but wonder *why* he kept smiling while his peers were so deeply dissatisfied, smiling even though he didn't seem to have anything to smile about.

Cypher is an easy character to hate.

He's sarcastic and kinda douchy. He betrays Morpheus to the machines. He kills those that thought him a friend.

But putting all that aside, there is something deeply sympathetic about Cypher. He's a bit of a loner and probably uses sarcasm as a shield. His feelings for Trinity are unrequited. He doesn't feel appreciated by Morpheus. He's tired of the fight, so tired.

So he makes a deal with the machines, relinquishing control of his life, content to let fate's winds blow him where they will.

He wants life to be easy.

It was not always this way. He, like the others, had been given the symbolic choice. By taking the red pill, Cypher chose life. It is a decision he lives to regret, one he spends the entire movie trying to undo.

Cypher was not The One, and after nine years he longs for the simple, artificial delicacies of the Matrix. But more than that, he wishes not to *know*.

Cypher: "I don't want to remember nothing. Nothing! You understand?"

It is said that nobody is truly dead until they are forgotten. Willingly sacrificing his own memory is akin to suicide, a death of the spirit and mind if not the body. By taking the machines up on their offer and going back into the power plant, Cypher throws his body onto the pyre for good measure too.

Cypher Rejects Life and Chooses Death

Cypher is not so different from the old grocery store clerks I once knew. Or, more recently, the office drones marking the days until retirement. They are all of them resigned to fate. They've given up their agency. If they live at all, it is only for some far-off tomorrow where everything will surely be better.

They have surrendered.

What leads to this death of the spirit? Why do some people quit when life unfolds differently than they'd hoped, while others remain unaffected despite similar circumstances?

Why did Rex keep smiling?

Morpheus is an enigmatic figure, with his mirrored sunglasses and cape-length black coat and that knowing, quasi-condescending smile. As Captain of the *Nebuchadnezzar*, he is responsible for the safety of the crew, many of whom he personally rescued from the Matrix. He holds the access codes to Zion and guards them with his life. But above all of that, he spearheads the search for The One, the figure of prophecy who will save humanity.

There is a lot on his shoulders. But you wouldn't know it from watching him.

Morpheus has spent years, perhaps the better part of his life, searching. Even after all the false starts and near-misses and friends lost, he remains committed to the cause. While the others express doubt, he is singularly hopeful.

He Has Found His Life's Purpose, And By Pursuing It, He Is At Peace

The world outside the Matrix is scarred and cold. It is a bleak place of nightmare, where humans are hunted relentlessly. It is a poor kind of reward for escaping. But unlike Cypher, Morpheus embraces this terrible truth.

> *Neo: "I can't go back, can I?"*
> *Morpheus: "No. But if you could, would you really want to?"*

Each person Morpheus rescues from the Matrix is first offered a choice, represented by those brightly colored pills: the truth, painful as it may be; or the lie, seductive and easy.

The truth represents a conscious decision to live. It will not be easy. You will have to fight, but it will be a life on your terms.

The lie is a poison, whispering that it would be better to remain oblivious, to let life happen as it will. The lie squanders life. It is death and decay. Too many people live the lie, going about their lives as though programmed, waiting for the carrot at the end of a very long stick, oblivious that it will be descicated and ruined before they get there. If they ever do.

Meanwhile people like Rex find purpose in their circumstances, good or bad, and in that purpose they find contentment, peace, joy. A central conceit of the film is the concept of fate and its role in our lives. Neo, a figure of prophecy, seems predestined to save humanity. It is a proposition he vehemently rejects.

Morpheus: "Do you believe in fate, Neo?"
Neo: "No."
Morpheus: "Why not?"
Neo: "Because I don't like the idea that I'm not in control of my life."

But Neo's not actually *in* control. Most of his life was spent unknowingly inside a computer facsimile. The first days outside the Matrix he spends learning, training, listening. He follows Morpheus, does what he's told to do.

The first time Neo actually exerts his own agency is when he hatches the plan to rescue Morpheus. Up to that point, he is merely a passenger in his own life.

Going up against the Agents is suicide, but by choosing that path, Neo has chosen life. And in doing so, he starts to believe.

He is no longer afraid of stepping out on the ledge.

He is living, for the first time.

Some very smart people think that we are probably living inside a Matrix-like simulation. Whether or not that's true, it is very easy to go about life as though programmed, lulled into semi-consciousness by tedium and repetition, looking forward to the next thing. Accepting the lies the world peddles. Seeking contentment in worldly things. Seeking, but never finding.

You may not believe in fate, but there is no denying that life will happen whether you participate or not.

We all have a choice to make. We can stay inside and let life happen to us. Or we can go out on that ledge, regardless of our circumstances. Take a risk. Live.

The Screams Of Women In Film And What *Twin Peaks* Can Teach Us About It

by Ariana DiValentino[9]

Walter Ong has said that "one cannot utter a sound without exercising power." In his book *Sound States: Innovative Poetics and Acoustical Technologies* (which was in turn referenced by academic Cristof Migone in his book *Sonic Somatic: Performances of the Unsound Body*), Steve McCaffrey quotes Ong. Apparently there's an agreement, within at least a certain tradition of sound and oration theorists, that making sound equals exercising power. On this, I wonder if any of these men have ever been made to scream.

Is it really always powerful to emit sound? Even when it's by the direction, or force, of someone else? The relationship between screaming and power is strong, but it's not consistent, and it often varies along gendered lines. From Hollywood horror to the auterism of David Lynch, the presence of the female scream signifies a power dynamic – often involving violence – between character, actress, director, and audience.

Thanks to the groundbreaking essay "Visual Pleasure and Narrative Cinema" by Laura Mulvey, the idea of the "male gaze" in film (and beyond) is common vocabulary for more than just feminist film scholars. The way that women's images are exploited onscreen is a recurring conversation in academic and popular culture. But as some scholars have pointed out, we ought to pay the same attention to the way the sounds, not just the images, of female and femme bodies play into the power dynamics of the medium.

---

[9] Ariana DiValentino is a writer, filmmaker, and et cetera based in Los Angeles. She is very, very worried.

To record sound, just as to shoot an image, is to produce it, not merely reproduce it, for an audience. The methodology of recording, as well as its treatment in post-production, determines what will be heard upon playback. The proximity of microphone to subject, among other technicalities, mediates the sound coming from its originary source. In "Speaking, Singing, Screaming: Controlling the Female Voice in American Cinema," sound theorist and practitioner Liz Greene describes in great detail[10] the way women's voices have traditionally been recorded in studio settings. Working under the assumption that women's voices do not bear the same air support and thus power of men's voices, microphones would be held closer, thus producing a more intimate sound rather than a more resonant one. In these cases, female voices are thereby not enabled to fill a space – literally, in the act of recording, and visually, within the images to which the sound is synced – in the same way that male voices often are. This produces a prevalence of whispering and otherwise soft-spoken female voices in film and music, which Greene poses as an example of the "male ear" (building on Mulvey's anatomy of the male gaze) that literally hushes women, preventing a filmic sound and image experience from being overwhelmed by a woman's voice.

Scream Queen

I would argue that this practice in sound recording and mixing even applies when women do raise their voices in film, particularly when they scream. Perhaps due to the gendering of emotions like fear and vulnerability, the prevalence of male screaming in film seems to be lower than female screaming. Comprehensive data

---

[10] Greene, Liz, "Speaking, Singing, Screaming: Controlling the Female Voice in American Cinema" Liz Greene Sound (2009) http://www.lizgreenesound.com/wp-content/uploads/2018/05/Speaking_Singing_Screaming_Controlling_t.pdf

on the prevalence and duration of terrified shrieking in film, by gender, would be enlightening, but in lieu of that, consider that the female victims of classic slasher films have birthed their own genre of actress: the "scream queen."

Despite the regal title, however, female stars of horror movies are exemplary objects of the "male ear" (and gaze) even when sound is recorded by more equalizing on set rather than studio methods. Female screams, even when shrill and enduring, tend not to "fill" space, either visually or within the soundscape. When a scream is accompanied by a close-up of the actress eliciting it, this tends not to be for very long and is usually bolstered by shots of her running or hiding within wider shots. Within the soundscape, the scream is rarely the only sound, or even a dominant one, for more than a few seconds. Typically, non-diegetic music accompanies scenes of heightened terror, as well as other diegetic sounds like footsteps. Through the post-production sound mixing process, the woman's scream merely becomes another object in the soundscape. Meanwhile, the monstrous, inhuman killer's cold silence represents his unshaken position of power.

Of course, the horror genre is by nature exploitative, depicting gore and its auditory counterpart, screaming, for the viewer/listener's pleasure. The character's terror is designed to be reveled in. And while exploitative pleasure need not necessarily exist along gendered lines, it tends to be, especially in classic slasher-genre films. Mulvey's seminal work on the "male gaze" outlines "scopophilia," or pleasure derived from looking, in its relation to the cinema and gender. The audience, typically presumed male by male filmmakers, marketers, and executives, enjoys the subject position in watching feminine spectacle – an object of their viewing, different from the presence of male actors with which viewers identify – on screen. And though when we usually talk about the male gaze, we're talking about women being served up in beautiful, sexy images for the erotic pleasure of viewers, that's not the only flavor scopophilia comes in. If there's anything that decades of horror movies have taught us, it's that for some reason (probably better explored by psychologists), audiences love watching a sexy woman get brutally murdered.

Film, of course, is an aural as well as visual medium, and as Liz Greene has quoted Kaja Silverman, the "female voice is as relentlessly held to normative representations and functions as the female body" (63). We film scholars, makers, and enthusiasts have not paid enough attention to this. The topic of "normative representations" is in part addressed by Greene's analysis of how the female voice has traditionally been recorded, but as for the question of "function," we might consider a phenomenon of "auraphilia," a term I use here to describe such function.

All of this is to say that just as an audience may derive pleasure from fantastic and feminized images on screen, they may also derive pleasure from fantastic and feminized sounds, whether or not those images or sounds are ones we think of as *pleasant*. A feminized recorded voice in film, even and perhaps especially when screaming, exists for the auraphilic pleasure of the privileged, silently listening audience. She is made to scream so they may hear. And when the auraphilia happens in the instance of screaming rather than, say, singing, we ought to ask again: is it really always powerful to elicit a sound? Or is being made to scream in a movie, as a woman or femme, more akin to being presented for the consumption of another?

David Lynch, *Twin Peaks*, and Hollywood Sound Tropes

Liz Greene turns to David Lynch's films *Mulholland Drive* and *Blue Velvet* in her exploration of the "male ear" and women's voices in cinema, but I'd like to talk about Lynch's series *Twin Peaks*. Lynch's body of work, especially the decades-spanning multimedia franchise that makes up the *Twin Peaks* canon, plays cleverly with sound tropes and technique, as well as the wonderfully messy dichotomies of masculine vs. feminine, active vs. passive, and good vs. evil. His use of all of these elements is complicated, ambiguous, and multivalent, which makes it an interesting case study for our purposes. It is not immediately clear if the many instances of women screaming in Lynch's work simply reproduce sexist Hollywood tropes, call our attention to them, or truly subvert them.

The series is anchored around the murder of well-loved high schooler Laura Palmer, known in town for her charity, warmth, and beauty. Through the testimonies of her friends and neighbors, we come to understand her as a paragon of goodness that exists/existed adjacent to extreme evil, situated similarly to the town itself. Violence against women is a central theme in "Twin Peaks," including the suffering and death of Laura as well as several other female characters. The nature of this violence is very different from that in a slasher film, wherein female characters tend to be so thinly written so as to keep the audience from developing much empathy for them and thus being able to enjoy the violence, rather than be horrified or saddened by it.

Compared to classic horror and other cinema as indicted by Mulvey and my own analysis, the role of women in *Twin Peaks* is more ambiguous. Female bodies are not hacked up in gory scenes for the spectator's horror-pleasure; in fact, most of the truly brutal violence happens off-screen. Also, *Twin Peaks* is an incredibly slow show, allowing us to spend far more time soaking in the atmosphere and learning about the wide cast of characters than in moments of intense violence. So while violence against women is prevalent in the show, it's not really offered up as a pornographic sort of pleasure.

This, in and of itself, is not necessarily feminist or subversive; depicting violence against women as common or fact, even a tragic and reprehensible fact, doesn't really do much to topple that power structure. But the nature of some of the most memorable screams in the series suggest a subversive possibility.

If you've seen *Twin Peaks*, you'll remember the Black Lodge, the strange, spectral dimension where characters' personality traits – good, evil, active, passive – are inverted. Laura's doppelganger, unlike that of other characters, does not escape the Lodge to wreak havoc on others. It's more a manifestation of madness than evil.

Real Laura is dead when we first meet her, and though we hear of some painful moments and confessions through other characters, she does not get to express her anguish before the audience. Even in a flashback to her murder that takes place in the second season, we only see her face in flashes – and its expression, more crazed than afraid or in pain, suggests a switch to or melding with her doppelganger. We do not see or hear Laura suffer the way we might expect.

Laura's doppelganger, however, makes herself heard. In the last episode of the original series, regular Laura, trapped in the Black Lodge, says to Cooper, "See you again in 25 years. Meanwhile…" Some time later, he enters another room in the Black Lodge and Laura's doppelganger, distinguished by her whitened eyes, picks up where she left off. "Meanwhile…" she repeats, then commences screaming. The screaming is more terrifying than terrified, seeming to express a kind of anger or frustration rather than fear. It is high-pitched and grating, and lasts twenty seconds. It is both a shriek and a growl, and it is not accompanied by any other sound or score. When it is happening, it is the only sound happening. Laura's doppelganger stares at and eventually approaches the camera. She continues screaming, mouth agape and cataracted eyes wild, even after Cooper runs out of the room. The scream is intended for the audience as much as it was for him.

We get the sense that the Laura that exists within the Lodge is the spectral part of her, the small force of good that accompanies the great evil. When Cooper asks her if she is Laura Palmer, she says, "I feel like I know her, but sometimes my arms bend back," possibly referring to the ropes tied around her by her killer. The "sometimes," however, suggests a recurrence. In one replaying of this scene that happens in The Return, she removes her face to reveal glowing light within. The Laura that exists in the Lodge is the universal goodness trapped within a net of evil. Her screaming double is the inherent frustration, anger, and necessarily failed attempt at agency that comes with being an eternal victim, an eternal site of pain.

But is it really failed? At one moment in the original series, Bobby Briggs, boyfriend of Laura, blames himself and everyone in town for knowing that Laura was suffering but turning a blind eye. She dies out of everyone's sight and earshot. Laura's doppelganger, or perhaps the doppelganger of the spectral force Laura embodied, makes us hear her suffering. We are forced to recognize it, and it's not easily forgotten. It would be challenging to say one might enjoy her scream the way one might delight in the dramatic screams of a horror movie heroine, because Laura's are so profoundly disturbing. Auraphilia is disallowed. The screams grip the audience in a very particular way and shake us to our core. Female suffering may be a part of life – even a part of nature – but Laura makes us feel it. She makes us just as powerless as she is.

Laura Palmer's scream is of such central importance to the themes of *Twin Peaks* as a whole, that it is in fact the last sound of the series. At the end of The Return, after traveling through time in hopes of saving Laura from her fate, only to have her sort of disappear from time and memory, Cooper finds another sort of Laura doppelganger, also played by actress Sheryl Lee: a woman who knows herself as Carrie Page. They return to *Twin Peaks* together and just when we seem to be at a dead end, the other timeline appears to show through: standing outside the house, we faintly hear Sarah Palmer calling Laura down for dinner.

Carrie Page, who seems in an instant to remember everything that befell Laura Palmer, screams in horror. The lights go out and the saga is over.

Despite changing the actual events of the timeline, the roles remain the same – even becoming an entirely different person does not spare Laura from being the one who experiences deep suffering. Cooper, despite going to extreme lengths across different universes, is unable to prevent any evil or pain. It seems female bodies (and souls) are destined to be the eternal sites of suffering, the masculine specters of evil unable to be truly vanquished, even if dark doppelgangers are successfully defeated or re-contained within the Black Lodge. It seems to be that the archetypes that make up the world are simply its unchangeable fabric: female suffering, male heroes pursuing good, and hypermasculine evil. None of the three can ever cease to exist – and so, Laura's scream penetrates universes, an eternal truth.

Making an evaluation of *Twin Peaks* as a sexist, feminist, or somewhere-in-between work is thus not simple. While it certainly paints the universe as dystopian, offering no escape from the horrific ways women are positioned within it, it does so with awareness and certainly does not invite audiences to revel in these horrors the way we might in classic horror films. The viewer is far more likely to be deeply affected by the disturbing and hard-to-forget finales of the original and revival series, both of which are punctuated by screams that linger in memory for years. Chances are, one does not simply turn it off and go to bed. It would probably be inaccurate to describe the series finales as something one "enjoys," per se. At the very least, we can credit Lynch for repositioning audiences in relation to female suffering, by subjecting them to its horrors, rather than simply subjecting female bodies and voices on screen to a male gaze and ear.

And maybe, for a work of horror, this is enough. Horror fans[11], writers[12], podcasters[13], film critics[14], academics[15], and probably your dad have all pointed out that horror, intentionally or unintentionally, is excellent at holding a mirror up to society and reflecting its most salient fears in the form of parable. It might be that a complicated narrative world, in which feminine life is always subjected to suffering, no matter how hard one man tries to change things, is exactly what our society needs to see – as much now as 30 years ago.

---

[11] Suebsaeng, Asawin, "Here's Why Your Favorite Horror Movies Are So Left-Wing," The Daily Beast (October 31, 2014)
https://www.thedailybeast.com/heres-why-your-favorite-horror-movies-are-so-left-wing
[12] Palmer, Landon, "Haunting the Suburbs: How White Flight Changed Paranormal Cinema," Film School Rejects (October 28, 2014)
https://filmschoolrejects.com/haunting-the-suburbs-how-white-flight-changed-paranormal-cinema-4d2f5c2d590d/
[13] "Halloween Special! Ed Gein and Slasher Movies," You're Wrong About Podcast (2020)
https://podcasts.apple.com/us/podcast/halloween-special-ed-gein-and-slasher-movies/id1380008439?i=1000465289930
[14] Currie, DiCarlo, Rachel, "Are Horror Movies Actually Conservative?," Independent Women's Forum (October 30, 2015)
https://www.iwf.org/2015/10/30/are-horror-movies-actually-conservative/
[15] Nelson, S., John, "Horror Films Face Political Evils in Everyday Life" Taylor Francis – Political Communication Vol 22, Issue 3 (August 21, 2006)
https://www.tandfonline.com/doi/abs/10.1080/10584600591006654?journalCode=upcp20&

Coraline and Freud.
Distinguishing Being and Semblance
by Timofei Gerber[16]

The turning point of *Coraline* occurs when she tries to run away from the Other Mother and the whole world around her begins to dissolve, leaving her in an empty white space. It is the moment where Coraline realizes that this parallel universe that she's discovered, and that was becoming more and more uncanny, is actually *fake*, artificial: a "small world." The blank and unfurnished emptiness surrounding her reveals that everything that Coraline has experienced in the World Within, i.e. the world of the Other Mother, has been aligned and arranged, towards and around her. The house and the Other Family that were initially presented as the inhabitants of an alternative universe, turned out to be an intentional and illusory construct. But what exactly is it that aligns and organises this World Within?

When we move into a new apartment, we furnish it according to our needs; similarly, the Other Mother's World Within is furnished according to Coraline's needs, or, more precisely, her wish for a perfect family. The World Within therefore serves as a wish fulfilment and everything in it is created according to this goal. Everything in it looks familiar; the house, the neighbours, and her family being almost exact copies, but *improved* copies, whose sole purpose it is to fascinate and captivate Coraline. The beginning of the movie establishes that Coraline feels neglected by her parents; the World Without, the 'real world', in that sense

---

[16] Timofei Gerber has an MA in philosophy from the University of Heidelberg, Germany, and an MA in film studies from the University of Zurich. He is currently writing his PhD at Paris 1 Sorbonne. He is also a co-founder and co-editor of Epoché Magazine (epochemagazine.org).

appears to her as a *world of deprivation*, while the World Within is to be understood as a *world of fulfilment*. This difference is illustrated by the picture of the boy that appears in both houses; the 'real world' version shows his scoops of ice cream having fallen to the ground, while the version of the 'fake world' shows him happily enjoying the dessert.

Coraline's wish for a perfect family is not created by the Other Mother, she rather capitalizes on it. Indeed, as the ghost children witness, the Other Mother feeds on children who feel neglected. On a family photo we can see Coraline's family on a visit in the zoo of Detroit. It is the picture of a happy family. But what's striking here is that Coraline isn't wearing her extravagant outfit— the yellow rain coat, the boots and her blue hair. This implies that the latter were a conscious reaction to the feeling of neglect, a typical strategy of children to catch the attention of their parents. This memory-image of the perfect family drives Coraline like a motor. It generates the regressive wish for a return to the family as it once was. It is therefore no coincidence that the Other Mother stages Coraline's entry into the World Within as a return: "Welcome home." This phenomenon, where a child acts as if it belongs to a surrogate family in which it remains at the centre of attention — a reaction against the changed family dynamics that occur when we grow up — was formulated by Freud in his text *Family Romances (Der Familienroman der Neurotiker)* from 1909. There he describes, how children, out of "a feeling of being slighted [Gefühl der Zurücksetzung]," develop the fantasy "of being a step-child or an adopted child"[17], fabricating daydreams that "serve as the fulfilment of wishes and as a correction of actual life."[18] Just like Coraline's nostalgia, this is "an expression of the child's longing for the happy, vanished days."[19] In short, the child wishes to remain a child, to

---

[17] Freud, Sigmund. Family Romances. In: The Standard Edition, Vol. IX, Hogarth Press 1959, .237; 235–241.
[18] *Ibid*, 238.
[19] *Ibid*, 241.

remain within the family's safe environment and its atmosphere of carelessness and joy.

But when it starts growing up, the child's role within the family, but also within society, begins to change; and the stronger it begins to feel said change, the stronger, potentially, its regressive reaction. The task of the child, as Freud describes it, is then to turn away from this wish; failure leads to neuroses, to a child in a grown-up's body that can't handle the non-familial experiences of reality. But how can this obstacle be overcome? In *Coraline*, the protagonist starts turning away from the wish once she gains insight into the artificiality of the World Within in the scene described in the opening paragraph. Not only is everything that Coraline sees and experiences fake, in all the 'wonders' that she experiences she remains a completely passive subject, a spectator. The neurotic condition is essentially an inability to act, as the subject is stuck in perpetual repetition — the repetition of its childhood. But not only does Coraline realize that the World Within is essentially *unreal*, it also is *confined*, and she can only remain there as a prisoner.

She realises that she needs to escape, for a failure to escape the World Within would lead to a complete integration into the latter, a complete schism from the 'real world'. This is what the Other Mother wants, and the decisive gesture for this total immersion is for Coraline to sew on the button eyes. Self-blinding, of course, is an ancient theme (Oedipus etc.). Symbolically speaking, it expresses an abandonment of truth (in the case of Oedipus an attempt to 'unsee' it). The truth for Coraline is the realisation that the World Within is artificial; 'unseeing' the truth therefore would mean to relinquish the ability of differentiating between being (truth) and semblance (artifice). As long as Coraline keeps her eyes, she manages to perceive the falsehood of the World Within; if she gave them up, the simulation would become total. The distinction between being and semblance would fall apart, a distinction that, in *Coraline*, corresponds to the two different worlds.

But what is it that distinguishes being and semblance? It isn't materiality, as Coraline is able to touch the beings and things of the World Within. For the differentiation we have two options: (a) the difference we've sketched above between fulfilment and deprivation; (b) the difference between openness and confinement. They both relate to each other, as they pertain to an overcoming of narcissism.

What does Coraline renounce in renouncing the World Within? It is the wish for the perfect family, but *not the family itself*. In fact, the happy ending of the movie is one of a return to the family, but through the abandonment of the narcissistic wish to remain a child. The child is in the centre of attention, it lives within the comfort of the family's care, and the family's task is (seemingly) solely to fulfil its desires. In returning to the family as a grown-up, Coraline no longer takes up the role of the protected child that lives in a fulfilled world. She steps out into the 'real world' that is indifferent her, and that therefore seems to follow a logic of deprivation. Religious conceptions can in that regard be seen as attempts to 'familiarise' the universe — the subject is God's child, just as it was for its family. Through such a parallelism, the subject can remain narcissistic, as not only the family seems to exist for it, but the whole universe. Following Freud, this amounts to an infantilisation of the subject, which is unable to face a world without purpose: "Men cannot remain children for ever; they must in the end go out into 'hostile life'".[20]

Yet, this 'negative' lesson corresponds to a 'positive' one that results from (b). The world of the family — or of religion — might be purposeful and warm, but it is also limited and confined. To fulfil Coraline's wish, the Other Mother didn't need to create a whole world, she only needed to create what is pertinent to Coraline's wish: her home and its immediate surroundings.

---

[20] Freud, Sigmund. *The Future of an Illusion. In: The Standard Edition*, Vol. XXI, Hogarth Press 1981, 49; 5–56.

Everything else, as we've seen in the opening paragraph, remains in the state of pure whiteness. The wish, then, will always create a confined territory that excludes everything that doesn't belong to it. If we wish for something, everything else 'disappears from view'. Its world is reductive and limited. The 'escape' out of the prison-like World Within would then not amount to a refutation of the wish, or of imagination itself, but of escapist tendencies of the imagination and of entities that promise a safe haven from the dangers of reality — be it the family or religion. Reality, as harsh as it might be, is at the same time vast and does not subjugate us to any metaphysical entity or structure.

The differentiation between being and semblance, as a way to separate the 'false' from the 'real' would then amount to sharpening our wits to perceive structures that try to trap and incorporate us into a machinery, and to find fissures where openness shines through. Imagination not only has the potential of entrapping us in artificial fantasies, but also of allowing us to act creatively in a world without a predefined meaning or sense.

The type of worldliness that is defined by a relinquishment of the narcissistic wish (i.e. of fulfilment), is established by Freud on a subjective level as part of any healthy coming-of-age, but also on the societal level — the renouncement of wish-based religion towards worldly science as he formulates it in *The Future of an Illusion*. This is part of Freud's utopian streak:

> *"By withdrawing their [men's] expectations from the other world and concentrating all their liberated energies into their life on earth, they will probably succeed in achieving a state of things in which life will become tolerable for everyone and civilization no longer oppressive to anyone."*[21]

---

[21] *Ibid*, 50.

The energies that are released thanks to science lie in the power to use nature as a resource to cover the basic human needs, but also of creating structures of meaning, instead of creating surrogate worlds like the afterlife. Just like growing up means overcoming the utopia of protected childhood, social maturity means overcoming the religious utopia of the afterlife (including secular structures that imitate it). The blissful happiness of childhood, as much as the serenity of religiosity are illusions to overcome.

The overcoming of the narcissistic wish — growing up — can be positively read as a liberation from an artificial and confining universe. The family keeps the child safe as long as it is small and helpless, but at some point, it needs to step out of it — and do what? Create its own family. What the child's narcissism hindered is its own future family formation; to become a parent, one ought to be able to consider oneself 'second', to sacrifice one's time and energy for one's child. This aspect introduces an ambivalent aspect to Freud's conception of the Family Romance, as the subject's escape, its growth, is acted out strictly within the familial structure. The subject leaves its family only to establish its own. It appears then that Freud doesn't overcome the familiarisation of the universe, and reaffirms it as a fundamental structure. This reflects the oedipal subject formation, where the relinquishment of the desire for the father/mother is completed by the formation of one's own family. Fairy tales— and structurally speaking, *Coraline* is one —often begin with a 'banishment' from home and end in marriage, where a new family is established. The adventures might happen in a foreign land, but in the end, they also have a function within the familial structure — namely its perpetuation.

Far from a liberation from hierarchical structures through the overcoming of the 'artificial' wishes of narcissism, Freud's conception subjugates the subject under the seemingly 'authentic' structure of the family. But it is a form of the family, which itself only produces subjects whose desire remains strictly on familial grounds. The subject desires nothing more than to establish its own family; and it is in that act that it finds its meaning in a cold world of deprivation. Growing up amounts to becoming a parent. This completely cuts the subject's ties to the world outside of family — to the social and political spheres. The mature subjects steps into the vast and open universe, only to recreate its own little territory, its house and home. It 'creates' its meaning by having children. Thus, the power structures that perpetuate the sociopolitical dynamics remain unquestioned.

The ideological character of such ways of thought lies in their naturalization of suppression, totalizing it and positing it as necessary and genuine. This aspect is concealed by staging the return to the family as a reconciliation of the daughter with her parents, of the subject with the "difficult situation" (ibid., p. 49)[21] — making us wonder, if not all reconciliation is a covert submission, or, to cut deeper, if not all radical differentiation between being and semblance, between naturalness and artificiality, is essentially a covert legitimation of a certain power structure. Just as slavery is legitimized by an apparently 'biological' difference between slave and owner, the bourgeois family with the paterfamilias is being posed as the only 'natural' constellation, excluding 'deviations' on the grounds of being 'unnatural'. The insight that said differentiation is subliminally based on power structures was worked out by Deleuze and Guattari in their book on Kafka:

"On the one hand, one discovers behind the familial triangle (father-mother-child) other infinitely more active triangles from which the family itself borrows its own power, its own drive to propagate submission, to lower the head and make heads lower. Because it's that that the libido of the child really invests itself in from the start: by means of the family photo, a whole map of the world."[22]

---

[22] Deleuze, Gilles; Guattari, Félix. Kafka. *Toward a Minor Literature*. University of Minnesota Press 1986, 11.

Asserted naturalness is always a positing of power, it is about controlling the subject, because what is natural is deemed unchangeable and is hence legitimized in its perpetuation. Naturalizing the family, its totalization, means that it belongs to an order of things that transcends the subject and that demands of it the repetition of the structure, one's own family formation within given roles and boundaries.

The shift that the postmodern criticism of Deleuze and Guattari attempted is one away from the division of natural/artificial to the one of open/close; instead of *normative*, it is now *topological*. Where are the exits, the passages, the stabilizing forces that delineate and judge what's inside and what's outside the territory? How can a territory be left and what hinders the escape? Subversion, as the two writers found it in Kafka, lies in an abandonment of the normative distinction — family is neither natural nor unnatural, it is a territory that includes and excludes and that follows specific rules. The question now is: what aspect of this territory leads to subjugation and how can the subject 'raise its head'? The resistance against suppression is not normative; it is reflexive and somatic, like a wolf forced into a corner. It is then not about refuting and refusing the family, and much rather about bringing to light what prefers to remain hidden.

Here, Coraline fails, just as Gregor Samsa in Kafka's *Metamorphosis*, for "Gregor refused to let go of the portrait of the lady in fur. He sticks to the portrait, as if to a last territorialized image" (ibid., p. 15)[21]. Coraline gives up on the family portrait, but not on the family; ultimately, she too is reterritorialized. When she escapes the prison of the Other Mother, she jumps right into the arms of the family. The movie ends, bourgeois enough, with a garden party. Reconciliation, the hallmark of the happy ending, amounts to an appeasement of the liberating impulses that initially fuelled Coraline's imagination — as occupied as it was by the regressive image of a lost childhood. The appeasing wisdom of 'no place like home' can be rekindled by a shift of emphasis, a slightly different intonation that reveals its nomadic potential; the *negation* of the very existence of such a place 'like home'. This is the first step of affirming openness.

Review: *Touch Of Evil*
by Julien Allen[23]

Touch of Evil contains a single-take tracking shot of such elegance and skill that it may one day come to be seen as the ultimate expression of Orson Welles's filmmaking prowess. See if you can spot it—it appears 34 minutes into the film.

It occurs in the apartment of young Manolo Sanchez, the chief suspect in the bombing of an American diplomat in a Mexican border town. It features, inter alia, Sanchez himself (Victor Millan), local police chief Hank Quinlan (Welles) and Mexican narcotics officer Miguel "Mike" Vargas (Charlton Heston). Observe how Russell Metty's camera, pinned in short focus, drifts slowly from the front room to the bathroom and back again twice, making sure to verify that there is no-one else in the apartment and no way in or out save for the front door—how it lingers on the empty shoebox Vargas replaces on the shelf, a shoebox which will later be found to contain two sticks of dynamite.

This is the long take as a narrative device, establishing a set of circumstances so that the central misfeasance of the film (the planting of evidence by Quinlan to frame Sanchez) can occur, and simultaneously exposing a tense, bilingual interrogation sequence as Vargas tries vainly to mitigate Quinlan's aggression towards the boy. It has the intellectual power and emotional intensity that only writing and camerawork of such subtlety can provide—and in its single take, the restitution of the entirety of the action within its own space and time.

---

[23] Julien Allen is a film writer and essayist from London, England. His work can be found in Reverse Shot, Film Comment, Cinema Scope and Senses of Cinema, as well as his own site, Orsonwelles.co.uk. He is currently researching and working on a writing project about acting.

The scene is all the more applaudable because it was filmed in the presence of a tetchy Universal executive, who had been dispatched by a panicked studio to find out why, by 7 p.m. on the first day of shooting, after ten hours spent only on rehearsals, Welles hadn't shot an inch of film. By the time this scene had wrapped, just over five minutes later, he had three days worth of finished footage in the can.

By 1957, Welles already had a strong inkling the game was pretty much up for him in Hollywood. Having returning to the U.S. after a long European sojourn, and between small roles in inferior films (*The Long Hot Summer*, *Pay the Devil*) and some TV Shakespeare, he had been cast as the lead in what seemed an unprepossessing potboiler based on Whit Masterson's pulp book *Badge of Evil* (despite the mythology, Welles considered the book to be "not that bad").

At Heston's instigation Welles agreed to rewrite and direct the picture for no additional fee. Like so many of his previous films (*The Magnificent Ambersons*, *It's All True*, *Mr. Arkadin*) it was ultimately taken away from him and "finished by others." Welles made a celebrated fuss on principle at the time, writing a 58 page memo to the studio demanding detailed restitution of specific elements of the sound, editing changes etc, a memo so detailed that it was later used by Walter Murch in the film's refurbishment in 1998. Yet, despite these public protestations, Welles was in fact more resigned than ever before to losing control of the project.

In the end he was broadly content with the resulting film and was even impressed with the Henry Mancini score the studio had tacked on. Murch's version successfully restored Welles's original intentions for the introduction (overlapping sounds of jazz music coming from each doorway the camera passes; no titles), but could not rematerialize lost footage, nor excise the two scenes between Vargas and his wife (Janet Leigh) that by their flatness, were palpably shot after the event without Welles's supervision.

In any case, none of these aberrations would do any lasting damage—we are far from the farrago of *The Magnificent Ambersons*. A film which was confiscated from Welles after mixed test screenings and butchered by the studio.

In Quinlan, the local folk hero, a policeman with an enviable conviction rate, Welles created one of the great noir heavies: a pachydermic, alcoholic, tyrannical racist brute who resorts to blackmail and murder to prop up his track record. The common comparisons—to Falstaff and even Gargantua—ignore the character's utter lack of joie de vivre.

To imbue a character as odious as this with tragic sympathy is Welles's playful way. Like with *Touch of Evil* itself, people tend to forget that Quinlan is seriously nasty—a personification of physical and moral decay. Yet when visiting his old flame, Tanya (an uncontracted Marlene Dietrich, filmed for the most part on a closed set to avoid the studio finding out lest they panic about her salary demands; her face lit as if in tribute to Josef von Sternberg), Quinlan melts and flirts, hinting at a past that might have promised more. "I didn't recognize you," Tanya says. "You should lay off those candy bars." Welles exaggerates Quinlan's deformity still further by having him speak barely coherently—a wildly unsympathetic, yet magnetic performance.

Welles was only 42 when he played him, retaining since *Citizen Kane* his propensity as an actor to represent ageing and degradation on screen. Despite the director's oft-declared distaste for what Quinlan stood for, Welles's film feels at times (especially in the final revelation that Sanchez was guilty) like a downbeat tribute to an artist whose magic has worn off.

The downright humorous number of similarities between *Touch of Evil* and Hitchcock's *Psycho*, released two years later (opening crane/dolly shots; the heavy as the lead; a feisty yet vulnerable Janet Leigh alone and terrorized in a motel run by a nervous madman; art direction – detailed interiors and use of taxidermy - by Robert

Clatworthy on both films; the use of natural lighting for outdoor scenes – *Touch of Evil*'s camera operator John Russell would turn DP for *Psycho*; Grandi's death-head lit by a neon flashing light vs. Mrs Bates' decomposing skull lit by a swinging bulb) actually serve to emphasise the real stylistic differences between Welles and Hitchcock.

Touch of Evil's justly celebrated opening crane shot contains what would become hallmarks of Hitch (especially the proximity of the bomb to the newlywed protagonists at various junctures without our knowing how far the timer has clicked down) but piles on top of this Welles's flair for light, sound and humor—and above all allows the camera to retreat from the action, to ebb and flow naturally, not to fix itself on the key subjects of the scene with impunity. (Hitchcock would eventually come up with his most Wellesian flourish in the slow, chaste retreat from the rape victim's apartment in *Frenzy*).

You can see the camera in *Touch of Evil* as a character in its own right, fitting for a film where the movement of bodies defines the personalities which inhabit them: Quinlan limps sloppily, creating movement only by the rotation of people around him; small-town hood "Uncle" Joe Grandi (Welles regular Akim Tamiroff) skips and capers like a clown; Vargas strolls at first with Heston's standard hard man gait (complete with the coolest sunglasses *that* side of Jean-Louis Trintignant's in Z) but ends up staggering, his body twisted into curious shapes, as he loses control of his emotions and embraces his own corruption; Dennis Weaver's night porter bobs unsettlingly, like a restless flightless bird.

The camera, for its part, glides and weaves around the other characters, occasionally hiding, spying, retreating behind walls and under porticos—like a silent witness to the sleaze and the dirty deals, but always, inexorably returning to the scene of the crime: the street. In this way the film delivers a powerful sense of location, which as the plot plays out to the end and we are transported past the oil derricks (lining the road like trees) to the bridge over a river full of detritus, remains one of the most intoxicating and resonant elements of *Touch of Evil* on the big screen. Venice, California stands in for Evil's fictional border town of "Los Robles."

As always with Orson Welles, we are never far from Shakespeare. Not just in the recognizable Shakespearian motifs (the washing of blood from Quinlan's hands, Dennis Weaver's fool/porter at the Mirador motel, Janet Leigh as Macduff's wife visited by a gang in the dead of night) but also in the sweeping moralism (the battle between law and justice), the layers of maleficence (Quinlan > Grandi > Sanchez) and the ultimate theater of betrayal and death.

Was there ever a more tragic character in fact, in all film noir, than Pete Menzies (played by Joseph Calleia), the loveable, slightly dim-witted acolyte who hero-worships Quinlan, colludes with him, defends him, finally decides to turn him in, then ends up killing him? Calleia's performance, by modern standards, outstrips even Welles's in its naturalistic poignancy—framed at one stage by the bars in the prison corridor, repelled by the spectacle of what Grandi's hoods did to Vargas's wife, he provides the film's beating heart. One soul, in that godforsaken place, which might have been worth saving.

If this satirical tragedy, marketed by Universal as a piece of exploitative trash and foolishly released as a B feature – a common way for studios to bury defective product - is primarily about anything in particular, it's about the morality of breaking the law in order to deliver justice.

When Quinlan snaps at Vargas that "a policeman's job is hard enough," Vargas responds "it's supposed to be—a policeman's job is only easy in a police state. That's the whole point captain, who's the boss—the cop or the law?" Quinlan on the other hand would seek to claim, like Raskolnikov in *Crime and Punishment*, that he can "march over corpses or wade through blood to do what's right," a view seemingly endorsed a decade or so later by Clint Eastwood in *Dirty Harry*.

Such a standpoint, left partly ambiguous by his romantic treatment of Quinlan's betrayal and death, earned Welles a brief reputation as a fascist (which he jokingly ascribed to the *Cahiers du cinéma* being full of fascists—and they had meant it as a compliment). You might prefer to see in Quinlan's fate, narrated over Vargas's short-wave radio in the final set piece, the awful culmination of a long struggle for recognition and respect.

Welles never made another film for a Hollywood studio—his own struggle continued to the very end. But he was some kind of a man.

Get Out and The Revolutionary Act of Subverting The White Gaze
by Dianca London[24]

Jordan Peele's film is an emotionally accurate depiction of what it means to resist and survive as a black person in America.

In *Black Skin, White Masks*, the Afro-Caribbean philosopher Frantz Fanon writes, "Ontology does not allow us to understand the being of the black man, since it ignores the lived experience. For not only must the black man be black; he must be black in relation to the white man."

The parameters of black embodiment within a narrative dominated by whiteness are limited. As a result, the complexity and depth of black masculinity is reduced to a static trope, as depicted through the laments of Shakespeare's Caliban, the compliance of Harriet Beecher Stowe's Uncle Tom, and the downfall of Richard Wright's Bigger Thomas.

When race is signified via the white gaze, narratives involving people of color are otherized. Their stories become tangential, contingent upon their proximity to or distance from whiteness. When the white gaze is privileged, all other identities are jeopardized, confining marginalized bodies to typecast tokenism or, even worse, erasure. Within this narrative scope, William Crain's Prince Mamuwalde becomes Blacula[25], a killer of his

---

[24] Dianca London earned her MFA in Fiction from The New School and her MA in English in addition to her MA in Humanities from Arcadia University. She is the former prose editor of LIT Magazine, a 2015 Pushcart Prize Nominee, and a Best Small Fictions finalist for 2016. She is a Kimbilio Fiction Fellow, a Callaloo Creative Writing Workshop participant, and VONA Voices alumna. Her words have been featured in Noisey, The A.V. Club, The Village Voice, The Toast, Lenny Letter, and elsewhere.

[25] Classicmov, "Blacula Intro (1972)," YouTube (December 27, 2011) https://www.youtube.com/watch?v=4XzQabdzAqQ.

people rather than savior, while the heroism of Ben — the only black character depicted in George Romero's cult classic *Night of the Living Dead*[26] — is cut short by a speeding bullet and a subsequent grave.

On screen or off, our culture's habit of centering whiteness suggests that black lives do not matter like the lives of white folks. But what happens when this dynamic of subjection is subverted? What happens when the white gaze is denied?

When The White Gaze Is Privileged, All Other Identities Are Jeopardized

Following in the footsteps of *Ganja and Hess*[27] and *Sweetback's Baadasssss Song*, *Get Out* — Jordan Peele's directorial debut — illustrates what is possible when the white gaze is subverted and its intentions are exhumed. Within this framework, Hess is immortal, Sweetback out runs the police, and Chris Washington (Daniel Kaluuya) survives a sinister weekend at the Armitages' suburban home. By placing Chris at the center of his narrative, Peele disavows the white gaze of its privilege. From the very beginning, he tears the veil between the reality of blackness and how it is imagined through the gaze of whiteness. The story begins and ends with Chris. His identity is the locus of the film.

Peele flips the script on the beginning to Stanley Kramer's 1967 dramedy *Guess Who's Coming to Dinner*.[28] Rather than opening with Chris and Rose — the contemporary stand-ins for Joanna Drayton (Katharine Houghton) and John Prentice (Sidney

---

[26] Multivinicius290, "night of the living dead part 10-10 ending.mp4," YouTube (September 9, 2011) https://www.youtube.com/watch?v=X6IDNqHuHmE

[27] Metrograph, "GANJA & HESS – Trailer," YoutTube (May 14, 2018) https://www.youtube.com/watch?v=qEM9oEKC1Ow.

[28] Thinker, Rational, Sane, "Guess Who's Coming to Dinner trailer," YouTube (July 21, 2009) https://www.youtube.com/watch?v=4a56FnhtuGI

Poitier) — en route to the Armitages' secluded suburban home, we bear witness to the brutal attack and kidnapping of a black young man. By focusing on capture and subdued consciousness, this on-screen image mimics a familiar tale to viewers of African descent. The first in a series of scenes highlighting the monsterhood of white supremacy, it also dismantles the expectation that cinematic tropes like the magical negro[29], the primitive monster[30], or the heroic friend[31] willing to sacrifice himself for the sake of the white protagonist will persist. This horrifying scene in the suburbs isn't merely metaphor and foreshadowing; it's an allusion to our nation's origin.

A similar allusion accompanies our introduction to Chris. As viewers, we watch as our soon-to-be hero stands alone in the bathroom of his New York City apartment. As he looks into the mirror to examine his face, his reflection reveals something rarely depicted by mainstream film: a non-sensationalized representation of black manhood and vulnerability. Unlike Rose (and her mother, much later in the film), the audience is instantly granted access to Chris's interior, a spatial avatar of his inner psyche. By doing so, Peele places Chris at the center of his cinematic universe; he is the axis that connects us to all that has yet to unfold. It isn't until he lets Rose into his apartment that Chris's perception of reality is antagonized, a perpetuated act that ultimately puts his life in jeopardy. From her deceptively sweet entrance to her maniacal end, Rose (Allison Williams) pays perfect homage to the botanical origin of her name while reminding viewers of the ways in which

---

[29] Seitz, Zoller, Matt, "The offensive movie cliche that won't die," Salon (September 14, 2010)
https://www.salon.com/2010/09/14/magical_negro_trope/.
[30] Gonder, Patrick, "Race, Gender and Terror: The Primitive in 1950s Horror Films," University of Colorado Boulder (December 1, 2004)
https://www.colorado.edu/gendersarchive1998-2013/2004/12/01/race-gender-and-terror-primitive-1950s-horror-films'.
[31] "Heroic Deaths" by Black Characters in Horror Movies," BlackHorrorMovies (N/A) http://www.blackhorrormovies.com/heroic-deaths-black-characters-in-horror-movies/

white women[32] have historically been implicit in the incarceration and slaughter of black men.

As Rose and Chris drive upstate for a weekend at her parent's home, it is Rose who is behind the wheel. During the trip she scolds Chris about his smoking habit and coyly suggests that he is jealous after she speaks with his friend Rod (Lil Rel Howery) on the phone. Many of these actions are seemingly innocent, but upon further inspection it becomes clear that her behavior is microaggressive. Her dismissive deflection of Chris's concerns and endless attempts to challenge his sense of perception are a mode of violence. Through these actions, she asserts her narrative as truth, clouding his ability to solely trust his intuition. Presumptively, she is Chris's ally, his defender, the doting partner, but as the film progresses, her true nature is exposed. It is an all too familiar scene for people of color.

Racism in this sense — as bell hooks suggests in *Killing Rage* — is treated as if it were a "figment of our perverse paranoid imaginations." Rose's opposition to and distortion of Chris's perception is a sinister reminder of bell hooks' illuminating origin of white supremacy: "[it] is rooted in pathological responses to difference." The more palatable version of her parents, Rose is a stand-in for the self-identified feminist ally who fails to acknowledge their own privilege and the ways in which their identity can potentially silence and oppress others.

As one might imagine, things get worse for Chris once he and Rose arrive at her parents's home. Soon after they park the car in the driveway, Rose's father, Dean Armitage (Bradley Whitford), insists on giving Chris a tour, pausing to gush over his collection of objects and mementos acquired from his travels abroad. In the kitchen, the two encounter Georgina (Betty Gabriel), who

---

[32] Board, Editorial, The "Black Lives, White Lies and Emmett Till," The New York Times (February 6, 2017)
https://www.nytimes.com/2017/02/06/opinion/black-lives-white-lies-and-emmett-till.html

in addition to Walter (Marcus Henderson), the groundskeeper, was hired to help care for Dean's elderly parents. "I know how it looks," he confesses to an understandably skeptical Chris. Dean then states for reassurance that he would have voted for Obama a third time, if he could have. Again, Chris's perception is challenged by semantics. Dean masks his true intentions behind progressive claims. In his attempts to gain Chris's trust, he camouflages his violent agenda with liberalism.

Jeremy (Caleb Landry Jones), Rose's brother, does the opposite. He arrives to dinner late, tells crude stories, and attempts to put Chris into a headlock despite everyone's vocal protests. A product of suburban privilege and affluence, Jeremey is unapologetically crass. He objectifies Chris's embodiment in a fashion reminiscent of an 18th century anthropologist. He is the id of the Armitage family, an heir to the mentality that W.E.B. Du Bois profiles in *The Souls of White Folks*.[33]

The Armitage family's matriarch, Missy, is initially the least threatening. She is a calculatingly calm voice of reason juxtaposed against the chaos of her son and cringe-worthy awkwardness of her husband's repeated use of phrases like "my man" and "thang." When Georgina accidentally spills tea onto the table, it is Missy who suggests that she go inside to rest. Of course the initial interpretation of each of these actions is undone by the film's climax, but before the Armitages' true selves are uncovered, she remains a lesser evil. Because of this, Chris's guard is down when he is around her, and although he doesn't accept her offer for hypnosis, he doesn't view her as a threat.

Like Rose, Missy attempts to overpower Chris's perception and his sense of reality by suppressing his sense of truth with the weight of her own. By placing Chris under hypnosis against his

---

[33] Bois, Du, W.E.B., "The Souls of White Folks," Harcourt, Brace and Company, (1920) https://umwblogs.org/wp-content/blogs.dir/5632/files/2012/08/The-Souls-of-White-Folk.pdf

wishes, she violates not only his body but his mind, thus becoming the celluloid representation of countless physicians whose unethical[34], unjust[35], and inhumane[36] treatment of people of color is often dismissed by historians as antiquated ethics rather than racism. Once Chris is under hypnosis, Missy deceptively taps into his childhood trauma, forcing him to recount the experience of his mother's death. Once his defenses are weakened, she sends him into "the sunken place." By manipulating Chris's emotions, Missy is able to temporarily suppress his mobility, but she underestimates his ability to perceive and interpret what he can see.

The Armitage Family Is A Symbolic Representation of White Supremacy and Its Methodology Within Contemporary Culture

In a way, the Armitage family is a symbolic representation of white supremacy and its methodology within contemporary culture. Through physical and psychological violence and violation, supremacist discourse and ideology attempts to dismantle the black consciousness by insisting that what we see and feel and experience as people of color isn't reality. It attempts to dissuade us from our intuition, that gut feeling one gets when a white colleague calls you by the name of another black co-worker or when a retail associate silently follows each and every one of your footsteps in a store. The depravity of the Armitages' violence manifests itself

---

[34] Vasquez, Tina, "'State of Eugenics' Film Sheds Light on North Carolina's Sterilization Abuse Program," Rewire News Group (January 30, 2017)
https://rewirenewsgroup.com/article/2017/01/30/state-eugenics-sheds-light-north-carolinas-sterilization-abuse/

[35] Wall, L,L, "The medical ethics of Dr J Marion Sims: a fresh look at the historical record," Journal of Medical Ethics (June 2006)
https://www.ncbi.nlm.nih.gov/pmc/articles/PMC2563360/

[36] "About the USPHS Syphilis Study," Tuskegee University (N/A)
https://www.tuskegee.edu/about-us/centers-of-excellence/bioethics-center/about-the-usphs-syphilis-study.

long before viewers via Chris are forced to "Behold the Coagula." By the time the family's annual party is in full swing, it is clear that his suspicions are valid and that Rod's warnings, although at times comically dramatic, are not to be ignored.

Before discovering the box of photographs in Rose's bedroom closet, it is logical not to trust her. Before Missy forcibly hypnotizes Chris, it is logical to be suspicious of her motives. Before Jeremy attacks Chris, it is logical to distrust his intentions. Before Dean auctions Chris off to the highest bidder — the prestigious art dealer Jim Hudson — it is logical to distrust his politics. Through the lens of the black gaze, each of these grievous acts is not outside of plausibility.

By grounding his narrative within the tradition of the horror genre, the trauma that Peele's protagonist experiences operates as the driving action that leads to the climax of the film, while also serving as a haunting metaphor for racism in America. It's a terror-inducing portrait of a nation whose founding fathers bought and sold African slaves for the benefit of their families's estates and personal gain.[37] Peele's film is an emotionally accurate depiction of what it means to resist and survive in a culture that never anticipated that we would survive or fight back in defense. It is an assumption that is synonymous with the narrative ignorance of the white gaze. It is the assumption that black Americans can be duped into dismissing racist behavior and its subsequent trauma via earnest allyship and progressive lip service.

Again, we are reminded of bell hooks, who wrote: "The eagerness with which contemporary society does away with racism, replacing this recognition [of supremacy] with evocations of pluralism and diversity that further mask reality, is a response to the terror" of whiteness. *Get Out* disallows this masking. Although

---

[37] "The Trouble with Teeth," George Washington's Mount Vernon (N/A) https://www.mountvernon.org/george-washington/health/washingtons-teeth/.

Chris is sold, subdued, and deceived, and his identity is nearly erased, it is the clarity and affirmation of his perception — along with Rod's intuition, Dre's ominous warning, Georgina's tears, and Walter's suicide — that disempowers the Armitage agenda. This can be summed up by Jim Hudson's chilling confession: "I want those things you see through."

The horror of the Coagula isn't just an act of erasure; it's the act of manipulating perception, of de-centering blackness and reasserting the age-old myth that whiteness is universal and deserving of privilege.

Get Out Reveals What It Means To Resist And Survive In A Culture That Never Anticipated That We Would Survive Or Fight Back In Defense

In the end, the Armitages' efforts are thwarted and along with their demise, the white gaze is at last omitted. In the absence of their deception, Chris survives. He and Rod (who arrives just in the nick of time) drive away into the night while Rose's home and her family's legacy is consumed in flames. Her entire generational line is wiped out along with Jim Hudson. Chris's ability to dismantle, deconstruct, and defract white supremacy and the solidarity he shares with Rod is ultimately what saves him.

Through artful storytelling and Peele's decolonized lens, *Get Out* exposes the white gaze for what it truly is: a pervasive threat to black survival.

How Documentary Film Became Entertainment
by Josh Rose[38]

The past, present, and future of non-fiction storytelling.

Non-fiction storytelling is one of the most exciting and boundary-pushing genres of modern entertainment. And it's only speeding up. Everyone — from commercial directors, to professional documentarians, to branded content makers, to everyday people — are getting in on the possibilities of non-fiction.

But that wasn't always the case.

In the not-too-distant past, the word "documentary" evoked thoughts of history films, biographies, and art pieces — more interesting than entertaining. Even using the word "film" instead of "movie" had a kind of intellectualized art house feel to it. In the best case scenario, it was a new story told in an old way, driven by small budgets and less access to the tools enjoyed by bigger studios.

Today, non-fiction is getting credit[39] for being an innovative category of entertainment every bit as exciting, engaging, and entertaining as feature film.

It's quite a story.

The Hero's Journey

---

[38] Josh S. Rose is a director and photographer, living in Los Angeles. Rose is the current artist-in-residence at the esteemed Los Angeles Dance Project, he is also a Leica Akademie instructor and has taught photojournalism at University of California. Josh's work has been published in over 30 magazines and hung in galleries across the world. Rose is a recent winner of the international Spider Award competition for Black and White Fine Art Photography. Rose got his degree in Fine Arts from U.C. Santa Cruz.

[39] Edlestein, David, "Edelstein: How Documentary Became the Most Exciting Kind of Filmmaking," Vulture (April 14, 2013)
https://www.vulture.com/2013/04/edelstein-documentary-is-better-than-filmmaking.html

Documentary film, of course, goes way back. But things got interesting for the genre in 2004, when Michael Moore shocked the world with his deep, investigative look into the Bush administration in *Fahrenheit 9/11*. His was the first doc to win the Palm D'or at Cannes and, in ways we weren't quite used to, the filmmaker played a role.

From there, along with the overall rise of investigative journalism and reality TV, docs turned up the volume as a force to be reckoned with. *Super Size Me* (2004) processed the fast food industry, *An Inconvenient Truth* (2006) predicted climate change, Sicko (2007) disrobed health care, *The King of Kong* (2007) went up a level in the competition doc category and *Food Inc* (2008) followed the U.S. food chain. Even 2010's *Exit Through the Gift Shop* and 2011's *Jiro Dreams of Sushi* were able to make commercial headway with independent-minded biographies, artfully achieved.

Suddenly, it wasn't just what non-fiction was saying, but how. In 2004's *Born Into Brothels*, director Zana Briski gave cameras to the children of prostitutes to get images otherwise unattainable. And in 2012's *The Act of Killing*, directors Joshua Oppenheimer and Christine Cynn turned the age old documentary technique of recreations into a political statement, enlisting not actors, but actual participants in the Indonesian killings of 1965–66.

A new era in non-fiction had arrived, and it was remarkably creative. But that was only Act One.

Then web-based experiences, like *Welcome To Pine Point* (2011) and *Bear 71* (2012), as well as Nonny de la Peña's VR-based *Hunger in Los Angeles* (2012) all pointed to how well-suited non-fiction was for new media. These early, experientially-driven non-fiction stories became not just new ways of engaging, but really posters for the best uses of new technologies.

In 2014, we witnessed the quick rise of the serialized true crime drama, with the highly-acclaimed *Serial* podcast (2014), Netflix's *Making a Murderer* (2015), and HBO's *The Jinx* (2015).

In 2016, experimentation in non-fiction storytelling produced films like *Tower*, which was largely animated, and *Kate Plays Christine*, which blurred the boundaries between reality and fiction.

Today, we're seeing non-fiction entertainment winning the Innovation Award at Sundance and leading the way in the use of new technologies — from the most immediate use of advanced tools, to the most boundary-breaking applications of everything from audio to VR to AI. But we're also seeing a special attention to story arc and character development in unscripted storytelling that is every bit as compelling as scripted films.

To get a little deeper into the current state of non-fiction, I tapped the shoulders of a few of the people in the midst of it right now — from those who make to those who support. Here are some of the major themes:

Zooming In On Humanity

Two recent buzz-worthy documentaries go on two very different road trips, but in the same direction. Academy Award-nominated *Faces Places* visits rural France with cinema's Agnès Varda and photographer/muralist JR, while *The Cinema Travellers* rides along with two showmen bringing the art of film in their trucks to the outskirts of India. Interestingly, in both films, film itself has a background role — but the main characters are decidedly and compellingly unscripted.

Riding along with today's most gripping storytelling is like a trip out of idealized fiction and into something deeper and more in-touch with humanity. Truth, as they say, is stranger than fiction. And today's filmmakers are willing to get as strange as they must for a good story.

In the documentary *City of Ghosts*, director/cinematographer Matthew Heineman embeds himself in a group of people who have escaped Syria and are being hunted by Isis. It's not the first time he's found himself deep in the heart of conflict. Heineman also shot and directed *Cartel Land*, where he placed himself directly into the midst of organized crime along the U.S./Mexico border.

During one particularly captivating scene in City of Ghosts, we witness one of the film's main character having an emotional breakdown. The portrait is so intimate and powerful, it forces comparisons to Martin Sheen's "hotel room freakout" scene in *Apocalypse Now*. Except this version is real life, giving it even more power than a fictionalized version of it ever could.

Heineman's own recounting of its filming reminds us of just how beautifully imperfect non-fiction can get.

"In that scene, he's shaking, and his clothes are shaking and he's smoking a cigarette. And all of those noises and even the rustle when he's grabbing the cigarette and the over-modulated sound of lighting the cigarette — that texture is actually what makes the scene work. I tried to shoot that as dynamically as possible to really feel like you were inside of his head and inside of his soul feeling the trauma of years and years and years of what he's been through, pouring out in that moment." — Matt Heineman, Director, *City of Ghosts*

At Sundance this year, one of the standout films (in any category) was Bing Liu's documentary *Minding The Gap*, which went deep into the lives of three skaters — Liu included — growing up on the outskirts of Chicago. Liu's almost impossibly-close relationship to his friends, both on and off the skateboard, tears down the wall between storyteller and story. In a similar fashion, Academy Award-winning documentary filmmaker Vanessa Roth's recent multi-part series on Netflix, *Daughters of Destiny*, took her deep into parts of India most of the world hasn't seen up close.

The New York Times said:

"Much of it takes place in classrooms and dormitories. But it's at its

best when it leaves the school grounds and follows the children home, into a harsh and unchanging world whose realities seem hopelessly at odds with the ideals of the school."

I asked Roth about filming in some of the world's more difficult and cramped locations:

"In Daughters of Destiny having a selection of cameras (especially the GoPro and Osmo) we used were wonderful because we spent so much time in very small, crowded homes, narrow side streets, the bottom of a quarry, in villages where we did not want to bring attention to ourselves, in low light, in no light, in 116 degree heat, traveling great distances by car and at the school where we captured movement and the energy of kids." — Vanessa Roth, Director, *Daughters of Destiny*

Intrepid storytellers like these, trained in the art of capturing humanity at its most extreme, are bringing forward stories with all the impact and emotion of a high budget Hollywood movie or independent film — but with no script, actors, or caterer. And audiences are responding.

The Appeal of The Real

As a society, we continue to tip the scale in favor of experiences over objects and companies that put good over profit. Even in my field, photography, the call is for imagery that feels only slightly more heightened than something one could take with their own cell phones. More and more, people are seeking out realism, authenticity, and truth... a territory owned by non-fiction.

This is putting demands on non-fiction storytellers all over the globe to go out and make a narrative of just about anything.

Again from Vanessa Roth:

"I'm being approached about very unique stories and asked for new

storytelling approaches that in the past would have been very difficult to get off the ground. It is exciting to be asked to think creatively and to have the support and resources to experiment more with style and format and subject matter — it opens up so many possibilities into getting to the heart of what we all want our work to do (in any art form) which is to move, engage and reach people." — Vanessa Roth

This sentiment was echoed from Bing Liu, as well:

"I think I'm telling stories at a time when this type of emotional reaching-for feels absent from people's everyday lives. And at the same time, therapy, trauma, masculine studies, and a slew of other internal-emotion-facing fields are becoming more accepted and prominent. So I believe more filmmakers are going to tell stories that allow us to get more and more 'inside' of each other's experiences." — Bing Liu

Still, making a movie (or story of any kind) is a deep, complicated, and difficult task. And there's still, especially in non-fiction, a certain journalistic responsibility to it. The filmmakers I spoke to seem to be taking that balance very seriously — learning to embrace a whole lot of new creativity while still bringing a rigor and integrity to it.

As Roth says:

"Documentary filmmaking is not only a storytelling or arts field; it is journalism. It is education. It is policy. And it is a reflection of people, events, places and ideas that requires research, access, and ethics. And has real life consequences." — Vanessa Roth

Which means that despite the often run-and-gun techniques of gathering footage, there's an entire industry surrounding the making of story that must support and take a role, too. And this, again, looks far different in non-fiction than it does in fiction.

Support, For Real

A distinct difference between the culture of feature films and the culture of non-fiction is the circle of support built into docs and independent films.

In features, there's a pressure to rely on what works, to reject risk. The lack of all that in documentary means that the surrounding communities of the medium work more holistically, collaboratively, and supportively. And risk is encouraged.

While many know Sundance for the festival, independent and documentary filmmakers have become intertwined with the Sundance Institute, which garners support through funding as well as creative support through workshops and a group dedicated to emerging technologies. The entire community of Sundance becomes an ecosystem for filmmakers outside Hollywood's machine. There are many institutions geared toward similar supporting networks for filmmakers. The Ford Foundation, Tribeca Film Institute, M.I.T., PBS and *The New York Times* are but a few big names supporting documentary filmmakers in a variety of ways, from funding to education to distribution.

This new relationship between those who make and those who support is paying off in getting avante garde and new creative ideas off the ground and in front of audiences.

Hajnal Molnar-Szakacs, Director of the Documentary Fund at Sundance Institute (disclosure: Molnar-Szakacs is also my significant other) explains:

"Over the past 4–5 years, we've recognized the vital role that art, experimentation and story play in ensuring a vibrant landscape of non-fiction work. The Fund has always sought to support the storytellers among us — adding new, bold, expressive, cinematic non-fiction to the list of projects we support only makes it more exciting." — Hajnal Molnar-Szakacs

This support from the industry, in turn, emboldens storytellers to follow their vision, breaking out of stereotypes and constraints of the medium. Molnar-Szakacs describes the expanded creative palette that the filmmakers they work with are employing:

"We talk about the use of metaphor, transcending set norms and revealing something about the world around us; whether it's something like Hale County This Morning, This Evening, Strong Island, Cinema Travellers, Unrest, or Risk — it's both the subject and the voice and artistry behind it that we are supporting." — Hajnal Molnar-Szakacs

More Impact

All of this growth is being fueled by the fact that non-fiction works are often inherently action-oriented. Tackling social and cultural issues (globally) creates its own gravitational force, pulling in everyone from philanthropists to politicians and from donors to makers. It's not uncommon to see films being financially supported through crowdfunding sites like Kickstarter, Indiegogo, Seed & Spark, and Slated. These are often issues people want to be involved with from the beginning, even if only as interested, impassioned and supporting patrons. The force of a community can be very strong.

The film *An Insignificant Man*, which follows an insurgent political party in India, faced government censorship until support from the community forced a landmark verdict that allowed the filmmakers to show their story in its entirety. Non-fiction projects don't just have audiences, they have supporters. And they aren't just stories, they are agents of change.

But none of this would be possible if the stories themselves weren't effective in that change. Which they are.

Errol Morris' *The Thin Blue Line* (1988) showed us early on that a film could have an immediate impact on social justice issues.

Today, Kirby Dick's *The Invisible War* is credited with having made a direct impact on the military's rape policies. *Bag It* influenced law makers to ban plastic bags. *Open Heart* had an affect on policy in Rwanda. *Bully* created a movement in schools. *Making A Murderer* released a man from jail and Jinx might put one in. And experiential projects are having real-world affects, too — *Collisions*, a VR film by Lynette Wallworth, is a standout project that has made a real difference in making people aware of an unknown history of an aboriginal Australians.

Where Does It Go From Here?

With so much wind at the back of non-fiction right now, the sky is the limit — but the following is where much of the discussion is focused:

Distribution

Distribution in non-fiction has always been its greatest challenge, but that's rapidly changing with the evolution of media. What used to be a linear path toward a one-week run at a movie theater (if you were lucky) is now a fairly creative suite of opportunities being lead by new players like HBO, Netflix, Apple, NY Times, and Amazon.

Emerging Media

We are just beginning to understand the roles that AR, VR and AI will play in storytelling, but it's clear those platforms are advancing every day, providing experiences that feel more and more real. And if the past predicts the future, it will be non-fiction that pulls us all forward. Already, VR experiences are bringing cultures together and revealing life in ailing parts of the country — not just to audiences, but to policy makers, too.

Branded Content

Corporations are seeing the light, too, as marketing dollars shift to digital and social media — every company is becoming a content company. The roster of agencies for developing short-form content has broadened and embraced non-fiction up and down the chain, from the creatives who concept to the production companies who bring it to life. In 2015, Ericsson launched a 61-episode documentary web series called *Capturing the Networked Society*, which told stories across 25 different countries and covered a range of topics, from healthcare to transportation.

Unapologetically Involved

As described, all signs point to a more involved role for storytellers. Bing Liu's decision to be both observer and subject of *Minding The Gap* is a genre-bending move that gives other storytellers a new way to bring meaning and creativity to their stories. In *Cameraperson* (2016), Kirsten Johnson, who spent most of her formative working days as a non-fiction cinematographer, turned her trove of footage into a memoir of her own creative journey even, at one point, literally turning her camera on herself.

Rise Of the Citizen Storyteller

We all have stories to tell. Today, the line between our daily lives and our ability to put it into watchable narratives is all but gone. Take the YouTube channel *Ryan Is Driving*, where a South Carolina cab and Uber driver records his conversations to the tune of 1 to 2 million views for his top videos. As one passenger says on camera, "*There needs to be a documentary of the shit that goes on in Ubers.*" And just like that, now there is.

Yes, truth is stranger than fiction. But beyond that — as more talented artists and storytellers like these elevate the medium — it may turn out to be more compelling, too.

This Magnificent Cake Pokes Fun At Black People and Gets The Belgian Congo All Wrong

by Jumko Ogata[40]

Belgium became its own independent territory in 1831, a diverse space made up of German, Dutch and French cultural and linguistic presence. It became a parliamentary monarchy, and the throne was offered to Leopold I, a German prince from a small territory whose connections to the British Empire would bring balance to the region and avoid conflict with the surrounding monarchies.

During the Late nineteenth century, his son, King Leopold II, became determined to possess a colony in Africa like his fellow European empires. In Adam Hochschild's book *King Leopold's Ghost* (1998), we learn how through a series of skillful manipulations carried out by the creation of philanthropist organizations, in 1885, Leopold was ultimately granted the Congo Free State as a private possession to be inherited to Belgium upon his death.

The Belgian Congo turned into one of the bloodiest and brutal colonist governments to set foot in Africa, unflinchingly exploiting the natural resources and inhabitants of the area. The presence of rubber vines made extraction much quicker in comparison to rubber plantations (which come from trees) and the colonizers enslaved the population of the Congo in order to obtain this

---

[40] Jumko Ogata-Aguilar is an AfroJapanese Chicana currently pursuing her undergraduate degree in the Latin American Studies program at the National Autonomous University of Mexico (UNAM). Her research focuses on race, identity, migration and the preservation of collective memory in the Mexican Caribbean, where people of African and Asian origin interacted and overlapped creating a complex and diverse cultural landscape. She has been published by Universidad Veracruzana, Vogue Mexico, Urban Ivy Co. and the British Council of Mexico.

precious material. Men were ordered to go into the jungle and fill a daily quota of rubber as their families where imprisoned as collateral. Those who failed to meet the high standards imposed by the government had their family members maimed and mutilated, including children.

This is the historical context of Emma De Swaef's and Marc James Roels's film *This Magnificent Cake!* (2018). Divided in five distinct chapters that follow different characters and their experiences in this territory It is a forty minute film that tells short stories that occur in or around the Belgian Congo during the late nineteenth century.

The film was developed with wool puppets and stop-motion animation, using natural-looking lighting techniques that make the audience feel like they're submerged in the scenes they are witnessing. The colors present a stark contrast between the cold European backgrounds and the tropical rainforest in the Belgian Congo, accentuating the differences between both spaces with the differences in the color palette in each region.

These well-executed visuals do not, however, save the dehumanizing narratives told in the film. Out of the five sections of the movie, only two are focused on Black characters, and both ultimately meet an untimely death in humiliating circumstances. The fact that the first story is about King Leopold II himself, sets the tone for this attempt at redemption for the white/European characters. We see Leopold as a sort of melancholy caricature, a quirky old man whose aspirations towards greatness are projected through his dreams during the night. We witness the moment he signs the consolidation of the Belgian Congo in 1885, in a scene that reiterates the brutality of colonialist and imperialist policies — the fate of an entire continent is decided in a Palace thousands of miles away between powerful white men. This moment is interrupted by something so absurd as Leopold getting the hiccups, and the group of men running to his side trying to suggest cures. In the filmmakers words:

"I think the way we do it with this kind of absurdist humor is a way of confronting the audience. The audience laughs and then they kind of feel uncomfortable about laughing. It's kind of an interesting tension to kind of create in the spectator."[41]

This made me wonder: — What audience is this for? Which spectators did they have in mind while developing these jokes and punchlines?

During Act II, titled "The hotel pygmy," we follow a man from one of the African populations popularly known as pygmies, who works at a hotel as a sort of bellhop — even though he has an ashtray on his head and stands in the corner as if he were furniture. We briefly see him speak to a family member that visits him and the chapter ends when he is crushed by a piano that fell from a higher floor. The other Black character appears during Act IV, titled "The Lost Porter," and it is a continuation of Act III, where we see a bridge collapse and a group of enslaved African people fall into a river. Act IV also treats the plight of the only surviving man in this group with humor — the moving moment when he speaks to the head of one of his fellow workers ends when he is startled by a noise and slips into the river once more.

Both of these narratives may attempt to lighten the situations as the filmmakers explained, however, as a Black person I was insulted by the humiliation they make these characters go through. In the brief time they are on screen, we only see them through the white/European gaze; they are never more than a side-note or an accessory that serves to develop the stories of their white counterparts. The film transmits a racist image of Black bodies in the Belgian Congo; for they are not even allowed their humanity. They may speak, or move on their own, but they are not in control

---

[41] Official, CartonBrew "Emma De Swaef and Marc James Roels: On Making 'This Magnificent Cake!', Youtube, January 14, 2019. https://www.youtube.com/watch?v=HBeH7Jo3kRs.

of their lives. people that invaded their territory dispossessed them even of their identities, turning them into caricatures as well as furniture (figuratively and literallly).[42] The filmmakers' explanation of their creative process helps us understand why these biases appear in their film:

"And of course, our country, where we're from — Belgium has a very interesting colonial history that's not talked about very often, at all. So when we started doing a bit of research into our countries' history we realized how much we didn't know about it and how much is swept under the rug all the time.

Generally we're attracted to these kinds of subjects that have a tension in it…we thought this was also a very kind of tense and ambiguous subject that would be interesting to talk about in a very interesting setting when people go to these colonies. Who is it who go there? What are their intentions? And how do they behave once they get there? We thought it was an interesting setting."[43]

The authors use of the term "ambiguous" is not clear, but it is strange to refer to violent colonization as an ambiguous subject, particularly when it was as recent as the Belgian Congo. It may seem like a distant historical occurrence to De Swaef and Roels, so it becomes necessary to place it in perspective; this territory didn't gain its independence until 1960, only 60 years ago. The creative process behind the film becomes increasingly problematic once we learn of the sources that the stories were based:

---

[42] Hochschild, Adam, "King Leopold's Ghost" Houghton Mifflin, Company, New York (1998).
[43] Official, CartonBrew "Emma De Swaef and Marc James Roels: On Making 'This Magnificent Cake!', Youtube, January 14, 2019. https://www.youtube.com/watch?v=HBeH7Jo3kRs.

"We constantly do research, so everything is based on archive footage, photos, we're reading a lot of diaries written by people, missionaries, back then. There's a scene where all these kinds of porters plummet down from this bridge... Those are things that actually happened. And the fact that they were all chained together so... when you read it in the diaries, they aren't considered a tragedy, they consider it more like an annoyance that they lost so much cargo. I always thought that this is a very strange kind of way of dealing with the fact that so many people have just died... its kind of absurd. So this kind of... this absurd kind of atmosphere and this idea that these people going to these colonies that didn't have any kind of moral boundaries... there was no one to police them, they could just kind of do whatever they wanted. And it just creates this kind of weird, almost like a playground for them, they considered it as a playground. And it's so absurd that there's this kind of dark humor that we were interested in tackling."[44]

Merriam-Webster defines "absurd" as "having no rational or orderly relationship to human life, lacking order or value" or "extremely silly or ridiculous." In this sense, considering the fact that racist and colonialist parameters have never considered Black lives as human, the absurdity with which the filmmakers portray their Black characters is not provocative, it is not an attempt to question the racist system these individuals faced during Belgian colonization; instead, it upholds it. This directly derives from the filmmakers willful ignorance. This racist view of African people could have been avoided if they had Black people on their creative team. De Swaef and Roels' vague statements about their sources on the era clearly demonstrate that they only read the sources produced by white colonizers.

While the circumstances of the era make it difficult to find documented accounts of the inhuman treatment of African people

---

[44] Official, CartonBrew "Emma De Swaef and Marc James Roels: On Making 'This Magnificent Cake!', Youtube, January 14, 2019. https://www.youtube.com/watch?v=HBeH7Jo3kRs.

went through in this territory told through their own, they are not impossible to find. Two Black men from the U.S., George Washington Williams and William Sheppard, traveled to the Belgian Congo in the late nineteenth century and interviewed many Africans about the treatment they received from their white colonizers.[45] So what motivated two white, South African and Belgian filmmakers to write and produce a film set in Africa during European colonization without including Black people in the creative process or as substantial characters in their story?

In contrast, the white/European characters highlighted in the film are complex, multi-layered individuals. They have highs and lows, they succeed and fail, and are allowed to explore their humanity in every space they inhabit (and invade) throughout the narratives. The last act, titled "The deserter", tells us the story of Louis, a young man who is terrified of entering the military, and thus, decides to run away to the African colony his country has acquired, a space he has heard is rife with opportunities for young men like himself. He ends up more scared and lost once he arrives, and the story ends with him returning home in a sort of fevered dream (a hallucination, perhaps) with his parents warmly welcoming him home, tucking him in into bed.

During act III, "The fate of Van Molle" we witness a man run away to the Belgian Congo with his family's fortune, spending it all on a large mansion filled with beer. It is during this act that the scene of the porters alluded to by the directors is mentioned. Van Molle drops food behind him on a wooden bridge and the enslaved man that is behind him slips and falls, dragging the line of men chained to him fall into the river. In the brief moments that he tries to hold on to the bridge, we see a single tear stream down his cheek, until he falls to his violent death. Meanwhile, Van Molle remains unphazed. The rest of the act focuses on this man in

---

[45] Hochschild, Adam, "King Leopold's Ghost," Houghton Mifflin, Company, New York, 1998, 10.

a cave within his mansion, where he befriends a snail with a human face, accidentally crushing it with a rock after some hours. Van Molle weeps inconsolably over the loss of his new found friend.

These stark differences infuriated me. The white/European characters were allowed to be fallible, to make mistakes, to be human every sense of the word. The world was their oyster, and they had adventures everywhere. Meanwhile, the Black characters seemed like afterthoughts. They were the butt of jokes, and there bodies were easily ripped apart on screen without a glimpse of compassion or emotion. Even though the directors/writers criticized the lack of emotion the colonizers showed when the people they enslaved perished violently, they emulated this point of view through their film. Van Molle's mansion has a fence of human skulls surrounding it, and we see him use a coat hanger who's hooks are made from (Black) human fingers.

The absurdity of the film resides in its complete obliviousness of itself. By treating every character with the same amount of humor, but a reduced degree of humanity for the Africans, the filmmakers ultimately perpetuated the racist violence that occurred in the Belgian Congo. Not only did they graphically show the horrors the white colonizers imposed unto them, they also killed the Africans point of view and ignored stories told by Africans themselves. They erased any possibility for the Black people in the story to be seen as anything but slaves, instead of enslaved persons.

This Magnificent Cake highlights the dire need for antiracism as a vital political standpoint, not only as filmmakers, but as human beings in general. While their intentions may have been positive, De Swaef and Roels perpetuated a racist point of view on colonial invasion.

Antiracism asks them — Why does the development of white Europeans have to come at the cost of African (and particularly Black) lives? Why are white narratives allowed a full range of emotions and complexity while we, as a people, are still perceived and treated as sub-human? More importantly, why must the lives of Black people — our bodies, our resources, our labor be the price for a better life for white people? Unfortunately, *This Magnificent Cake!* misses the opportunity to explore their question with depth and seriousness.

Break Up the Media Giants
by Paris Marx[46]

The streaming wars will produce a new oligopoly. We can do better.

For decades, corporate consolidation has been judged almost exclusively on whether it would raise prices for consumers, ignoring how the market power of massive conglomerates can have broader negative effects on society and the economy. That's finally starting to change.

In the past year, the campaign to break up the tech giants has gained steam with support from Elizabeth Warren[47], Bernie Sanders[48], and other progressive politicians. Two-thirds of Americans now support the proposal[49], recognizing that monopolistic control of digital platforms and services has negative implications for privacy and economic prosperity. But we must also recognize that tech is just one part of a larger economic disease, and if it's truly to be addressed, antitrust regulators will need to look beyond the core businesses of Apple, Amazon, Facebook, and Google.

Given the media's importance in informing us about current events and crafting the stories through which we understand the world, regulators must address how film and television is dominated by a small number of media giants that are gaining ever

---

[46] Paris Marx is a socialist writer and host of Tech Won't Save Us, a left-wing tech podcast. Their work has appeared in NBC News, CBC News, Toronto Star, OneZero, Jacobin Magazine, and Tribune Magazine. Paris holds a Master's degree from McGill University and is writing a book for Verso Books due out in 2022.

[47] Warren, Team, "Here's how we can break up Big Tech," Medium (March 8, 2019) https://medium.com/@teamwarren/heres-how-we-can-break-up-big-tech-9ad9e0da324c.

[48] Lima, Cristiano, "Bernie Sanders says he would 'absolutely' try to break up Facebook, Google, Amazon," Politico (July 16, 2019) https://www.politico.com/story/2019/07/16/bernie-sanders-facebook-google-amazon-1416786.

[49] Stewart, Emily, "Poll: Two-thirds of Americans want to break up companies like Amazon and Google," *Vox* (September 18, 2019) https://www.vox.com/policy-and-politics/2019/9/18/20870938/break-up-big-tech-google-facebook-amazon-poll.

more control over the production and distribution of entertainment. The industry is undergoing an important transformation as the delivery of content shifts to digital streaming services. While that's generating new competition in the short term, it will result in further consolidation and less diversity in the long term — unless someone takes action.

Tech's Impact On Media

Tech companies have been engaging with media for a long time. Music was central to Apple's success, beginning with the iPod. Amazon made its name delivering books before selling us just about everything else. And Google has been scanning books, delivering music videos, and more for years. What has changed isn't tech companies' interest in media, but the scale of their ambitions.

All the major tech companies are creating their own content to make their services more attractive to consumers, competing directly with traditional media companies whose products they've long sold or showcased. Netflix was the successful pioneer, shifting from DVD by mail[50] to streaming, and realizing that high-quality, exclusive content would be key to drawing an audience. Amazon followed with its Prime Video service, Google with YouTube Red, Facebook with Watch, and now Apple is joining the fray with TV+[51]. Those services are competing with an array of streaming services from traditional media companies, including Hulu, CBS All Access, and the forthcoming Disney+[52] and Peacock, but tech companies have an advantage.

---

[50] Raab, Mike, "The Tricky Business of Media and Entertainment Tech," *OneZero* (October 14, 2019) https://onezero.medium.com/the-tricky-business-of-media-and-entertainment-tech-dd93f2b7d45f.
[51] Raab, Mike, "What Is Apple's TV Plus Strategy?," OneZero (September 11, 2019) https://onezero.medium.com/what-is-apples-tv-plus-strategy-d7c7bb10ea2f.
[52] Ravenscraft, Eric, "Why Disney+ Will Win the Streaming Wars," OneZero (October 15, 2019) https://onezero.medium.com/why-disney-will-win-the-streaming-wars-a7072acb0ffb.

In a recent piece about WeWork[53], Recode's Rani Molla explained how companies that masquerade as "tech," despite operating in traditional industries, give investors the impression that their margins and growth will be much greater than they can actually deliver, opening the venture capital floodgates. Once investors realize they're not going to get the returns they expected, however, it's already too late: The well-capitalized "tech" company has already crippled or wiped out its traditional competitors that couldn't benefit from a misleading tech designation.

While Amazon, Apple, Facebook, and Google subsidize their media plays with profits from other businesses, Netflix has benefited from this effect by painting a business that depends on high-quality content to bring in subscribers as being about tech first and foremost. That branding then eases its access to capital to fund its slate of original programming with massive annual losses, which, in turn, has placed significant pressure on traditional media companies.

The Changing Media Landscape

In recent years, we've seen a spate of massive media mergers that kicked off with Comcast's acquisition of NBCUniversal in 2009, but it has only accelerated since then. Disney acquired Marvel in 2009, Lucasfilm in 2012, and then bought out one of its main competitors[54], 21st Century Fox, in 2018. AT&T picked up DirectTV in 2015, followed by Time Warner in 2016, which includes HBO, CNN, DC Entertainment, and Warner Brothers.

---

[53] Molla, Rani, "What does it even mean to be a tech company in 2019?," *Vox* (August 16, 2019)
https://www.vox.com/recode/2019/8/16/20805770/tech-company-meaning-2019-ipo-wework.

[54] VanDerWerff, Emily, "Here's what Disney owns after the massive Disney/Fox merger," *Vox* (March 20, 2019)
https://www.vox.com/culture/2019/3/20/18273477/disney-fox-merger-deal-details-marvel-x-men.

Then, in August 2019, CBS and Viacom announced they'd be merging once again.[55]

Not all of these mergers were driven by streaming and Netflix. Disney, in particular, has been pursuing a content strategy reliant on blockbuster media properties that has allowed it to dominate the film industry in a way no company has since MGM in the first half of the 20th century[56], before the Department of Justice enforced antitrust laws against the major studios. But the mergers from the past few years are clearly motivated by a desire to bolster the content libraries of key traditional players in order to compete in the coming streaming wars — and it likely won't end here.

Ben Swinburne, Morgan Stanley's head of media policy research, told the Financial Times[57] that the media business "is getting harder, requiring more capital, more global distribution and ultimately more consolidation" — all trends being fueled by tech's entry into the space. Swinburne thinks more consolidation is coming to the sector as the ever-larger media conglomerates buy up smaller content players that haven't yet been snatched up, like Lionsgate and Discovery, and production costs are soaring as well.

Netflix, in its competition with HBO to create "prestige" television, has already significantly bid up production budgets[58] to between $5 million and $7 million per hour of programming, but as even more well-financed tech companies move in, they're going

---

[55] Alexander, Julia, "CBS and Viacom are merging to become ViacomCBS," *The Verge* (August 13, 2019)
https://www.theverge.com/2019/8/13/20746894/cbs-viacom-merger-acquisition-all-access-mtv-bet-streaming-value.
[56] Vary, B., Adam, "Disney Won. Now What?," *BuzzFeed* (July 3, 2019)
https://www.buzzfeednews.com/article/adambvary/disney-hollywood-20th-century-fox-marvel-outlook.
[57] Nicolaou, Anna, "A second wave of media M&A is coming," Financial Times (August 7, 2019)
https://www.ft.com/content/9629af48-b8b3-11e9-8a88-aa6628ac896c.
[58] Ryan, Maureen, Littleton, Cynthia, "TV Series Budgets Hit the Breaking Point as Costs Skyrocket in Peak TV Era," Variety (September 26, 2017)
https://variety.com/2017/tv/news/tv-series-budgets-costs-rising-peak-tv-1202570158/.

even higher. Apple, for example, is spending more per episode[59] on its U.S. talk show drama The Morning Show than HBO paid for the final season of Game of Thrones, which cost $15 million per episode, and Amazon's television series based on The Lord of the Rings is expected to be the most expensive ever made[60] — all while content budgets are still going up.[61]

The trends of greater consolidation and escalating budgets may seem like relatively recent developments resulting from the advent of a new technology — streaming video — but that's not the case. Looking at the history of media regulation shows that it's part of a longer process that could also inform the solution.

The First Wave of Consolidation

Before the 1990s, there were strict regulations on what the three major broadcast networks — ABC, CBS, and NBC — could air in prime time. The Financial Syndication and Interest, or "fin-syn," rules were established in 1970 because the networks' control over distribution allowed them to demand punitive terms from production companies.

Deficit financing was the primary way to produce television programming, which meant the production company made the show at a loss and hoped to recoup its investment later. The license for first-run distribution—essentially the first few times the show aired—often went to one of the major networks and covered most

---

[59] Nicolaou, Anna, Bradshaw, Tim, "Apple splashes $6bn on new shows in streaming wars," *Financial Times* (August 19, 2019) https://www.ft.com/content/4f7f4326-c2bf-11e9-a8e9-296ca66511c9.
[60] Siegel, Tatiana, "Inside Amazon's $250M 'Lord of the Rings' Deal: "It's Very Much a Creature of the Times"," Hollywood Reporter (April 5, 2018) https://www.hollywoodreporter.com/live-feed/how-lord-rings-tv-series-landed-at-amazon-not-netflix-1099213.
[61] Schedeen, Jesse, "Here's How Much Money Netflix Spends on Content Compared to Disney," *IGN* (October 15, 2019) https://www.ign.com/articles/2019/08/08/disney-outspending-netflix-streaming-original-content-budget.

but not all of the production cost. The rest of the cost and any profit came from the second-run and foreign licenses. Amanda Lotz, professor at the Queensland University of Technology, explains that this model shifted risk from the network to the producer[62] and incentivized the creation of large production companies that could shoulder the losses if a show wasn't popular.

The networks went further, however, and used their market power to demand a cut of the profits, so production company had to pay to make the show and give a cut of all revenue after the first run to the network. This arrangement, Lotz writes, "shielded the networks from risk but also enabled them to share in the reward of hits," and it nearly killed independent production, which fell from 33% in 1958 to 5% of all productions in 1968.

The fin-syn rules recognized that the networks were abusing their power and barred them from airing programming they owned in prime time or syndicated programming they had a financial stake in. Independent production rebounded, but the situation didn't last for long. Cable television started taking off, and a fourth broadcast network, Fox, was launched in 1986. Those developments allowed the broadcasters to argue that there was sufficient competition, and they had a sympathetic ear.

After Ronald Reagan became president in 1981, deregulation was in the air. The fin-syn rules were weakened through the 1980s before a full repeal in the mid-1990s. However, the promise that deregulation would usher in a new wave of competition did not come to pass. Lotz notes that just five years after the rules were repealed, "CBS held an interest in or owned 68% of its prime-time schedule, and Fox owned 71%." Instead of competition, there was a push to vertically integrate as networks increased their control of production to own their programming, making production

---

62 Lotz, D., Amanda, "Teasing apart television industry disruption: consequences of meso-level financing practices before and after the US multiplatform era.," *Media, Culture & Society* (August 2019) https://journals.sagepub.com/doi/full/10.1177/0163443719863354.

budgets soar from $1.2 million for an hour-long show in the late 1990s to $3 million in the early 2000s.

In 1997, Thomas Streeter[63] observed that "the cable fable is a story of repeated utopian high hopes followed by repeated disappointments… Cable was to end television oligopoly; instead it has merely provided an arena for the formation of a new oligopoly." The experience of deregulation should serve as a warning for streaming's effect on the media industry: It's not ushering in a new era of competition, but swapping one oligopoly for another as consolidation and higher production costs further raise the barrier to entry and increase the market power of dominant players.

Combating The Streaming Oligopoly

For now, there are a number of streaming services for people to choose from, controlled by either a tech giant or a media conglomerate that's trying to compete with some combination of large content libraries[64], popular shows like Friends and The Office, and expensive new series that are sending production budgets into the stratosphere to draw in customers. This situation won't last forever, and that's what we need to prepare for.

In "Platform Power and Policy in Transforming Television Markets," Belgian scholars Tom Evens and Karen Donders explain that streaming offers broadcast networks the opportunity to cut out the cable company and go straight to the consumer, capturing a ton of data on them in the process. But while there's some competition between them now, consumer choices will lessen as streaming matures for a very simple reason: "Platform markets

---

[63] Streeter, Thomas, "Blue Skies and Strange Bedfellows: the Discourse of Cable Television," *The Revolution Wasn't Televised Sixties Television and Social Conflict* (1997) https://www.uvm.edu/~tstreete/newfable.htm.
[64] Sperling, Nicole, "NBCUniversal Introduces Peacock, Its New Streaming Service," *The New York Times* (September 17, 2019) https://www.nytimes.com/2019/09/17/business/media/peacock-nbcuniversal-streaming.html.

are generally winner-takes-all markets and are populated by a few super-platforms."

Search is dominated by Google, e-commerce by Amazon, online auctions by eBay, payments by PayPal, ride hailing by Uber and Lyft, social media by Facebook — I could go on, but I think you get the point. And there's little reason to believe media platforms would operate any differently. If regulators don't take any action, we'll just end up with a few streaming silos filled with content owned by whichever conglomerate owns the platform as they continue to consolidate. But it doesn't have to be like that.

To end the capture of the industry by a small number of massive conglomerates, we should learn from previous media regulations. The fin-syn rules significantly restricted the ability of networks to broadcast their own content, forcing them to rely on independent production companies instead of vertically integrating. In film, a landmark antitrust case produced the Paramount Consent Decrees in 1948, ending the oligopoly of the major studios by restricting how they sold their films[65] and effectively barring them from owning theaters. They are set to expire in 2022.[66]

Both of those rules recognize that there should be a separation between the makers of content and the means through which content reaches its audience. As such, the ability of major companies to own streaming platforms and the content that populates them is against the spirit of those restrictions. To foster a better media ecosystem, regulators must renew and expand those rules for the digital era.

---

[65] Price, Philip, Vialva, Christian, "Your Entry-Level Talent Needs A Strong Frontline Manager," *Forbes* (September 17, 2019) https://www.forbes.com/sites/gradsoflife/2019/09/17/your-entry-level-talent-needs-a-strong-frontline-manager/#574a4f6c2356.

[66] Johnson, Ted, "Federal judge gives greenlight to termination of paramount consent decrees," *Deadline* (August 7, 2020) https://deadline.com/2020/08/paramount-consent-decrees-justice-department-2-1203007221/.

Reining In The Media Conglomerates

The problem isn't that regulators aren't concerned about the effect of massive companies on the media industry, but that the scope of their response has been too narrow. For example, when Comcast bought NBCUniversal, conditions stopped it from favoring its own content and withholding content from smaller distributors. Those restrictions have now expired, however, raising concerns about anticompetitive behavior[67], and streaming wasn't even a factor. To meet the challenge, regulators must get bolder.

In her landmark essay, "Amazon's Antitrust Paradox," Columbia Law School fellow Lina Khan suggested several remedies to rein in platform monopolies[68]: revising rules on predatory pricing to reflect the reality of platform economics, placing restrictions on vertical integration that would ban "a dominant firm from entering any market that it already serves as a platform," and regulating platforms as public utilities to relieve any concern they could "unfairly advantage [their] own business or unfairly discriminate among platform users to gain leverage or market power."

> *A more explicit rule stopping tech companies from sprawling into so many unrelated industries should be considered.*

What would those rules mean for media? Apple's decision to make TV+ just $4.99 or free with a hardware purchase[69] and Amazon's decision to bundle Prime Video with its larger Prime

---

[67] Manning, Rick, "Big Media Consolidation Presents Big Problems," *Investors Business Daily* (July 10, 2018)
https://www.investors.com/politics/commentary/media-mergers-problems/.
[68] Khan, M., Lina, "Amazon's Antitrust Paradox," *The Yale Law Journal* Vol 126, No. 3 (January 2017)
https://www.yalelawjournal.org/article/amazons-antitrust-paradox.
[69] Marx, Paris, "Apple TV+ is All About Selling More iPhones," *Medium – The Startup* (September 12, 2019)
https://medium.com/swlh/apple-tv-is-all-about-selling-more-iphones-f9d06c295da4.

membership could be seen as predatory pricing that provides those services with an unfair advantage. Meanwhile, restrictions on vertical integration would, in effect, stop platform operators from being able to produce their own content and force them to rely on independent production companies. That means Disney wouldn't be able to have its own streaming platform and could also be forced to separate its broadcast arm, ABC, from content production. However, a more explicit rule stopping tech companies from sprawling into so many unrelated industries should be considered.

If platform owners were allowed to keep making their own content, public utility regulation would ensure Netflix couldn't give its originals a prominent spot on the home screen or tweak its algorithm to give them a boost. It would be similar to net neutrality rules for internet providers, restricting them from privileging certain providers or content over others. Evens and Donders suggest this could also involve regulating prices and making the algorithm open access, while Democracy Collaborative fellow Dan Hind has proposed the creation of a cooperative media platform[70] to act as a public alternative, updating the public broadcaster for the 21st century. This would be the ultimate step to ensure content is fairly distributed, data is used ethically, and public goals are prioritized over what's profitable.

We're headed toward a future where entertainment is further monopolized[71] by a small number of massive global conglomerates with streaming platforms filled with content they own, making it harder and harder for small companies and perspectives that

---

[70] Hind, Dan, "The British Digital Cooperative, A New Model Public Sector Institution," *Common Wealth* (September 20, 2019) https://www.common-wealth.co.uk/reports/the-british-digital-cooperative-a-new-model-public-sector-institution.

[71] Raab, Mike, "The TV Subscriptions You'll Need to Watch Your Favorite Shows," *OneZero* (August 6, 2019) https://onezero.medium.com/the-tv-subscriptions-youll-need-to-watch-your-favorite-shows-9357eb1245fa.

aren't so easy to commercialize to have a shot. Right now, we're in a sweet spot where competition between the conglomerates is providing some of those opportunities, but history shows us it will not last — and it may already be ending.

Erin Schiffer, CEO of the Patriarch Organization consultancy firm, says the "golden age of streaming" is already over.[72] That's clearly evident when looking at Netflix, which was once lauded for offering creators unparalleled freedom, but is now being called out for making decisions based on an opaque algorithm[73], disproportionately canceling series created by women[74], and its business calculation to cancel series after just two or three seasons[75] to avoid the bonuses and salary increases that are expected for a successful series.

It can be hard to imagine any other way to organize the film and television industries given that we're used to their present structure. Still, looking at the past shows us that they've been composed in different ways at various times, and that restrictions can help put the public interest first and give independent companies room to grow. The appetite for antitrust appears to be growing, with both Elizabeth Warren[76] and Bernie Sanders[77] calling for action to address media consolidation.

---

[72] Alexander, Julia, "Netflix needs to grow, but it's sacrificing great original series to do so," *The Verge* (August 12, 2019)
https://www.theverge.com/2019/8/12/20791602/netflix-canceled-shows-originals-tuca-bertie-oa-streaming-wars-disney.

[73] Feldberg, Isaac, "Netflix's Cancellation of 'Tuca & Bertie' Renews Criticism of Its Perplexing Algorithm," *Fortune* (July 25, 2019)
https://fortune.com/2019/07/25/netflix-cancels-tuca-and-bertie-algorithm/.

[74] Travers, Ben, "Netflix Has Canceled Eight Series From Women Creators in 2019 (So Far)," *IndieWire* (August 6, 2019)
https://www.indiewire.com/2019/08/netflix-canceled-series-women-creators-2019-the-oa-tuca-and-bertie-1202163456/.

[75] Jarvey, Natalie, Netflix Under Pressure: Can a Hollywood Disruptor Avoid Getting Disrupted?," *Hollywood Reporter* (August 8, 2019)
https://www.hollywoodreporter.com/features/netflix-at-a-crossroads-hollywoods-dominant-disrupter-adjusts-growing-pains-1229618.

[76] Warren, Elizabeth, Twitter
https://twitter.com/ewarren/status/1162074257393893378?s=20.

[77] Sanders, Bernie, "Op-Ed: Bernie Sanders on his plan for journalism," *Columbia Journalism Review* (August 26, 2019)
https://www.cjr.org/opinion/bernie-sanders-media-silicon-valley.php.

Make no mistake: Antitrust action and the development of cooperative alternatives would completely upend the streaming wars. It can't come soon enough.

TCM Diary: Jane Fonda In the 1960s

by Beatrice Loayza[78]

In the November 1960 issue of *Pageant* magazine, a bright-eyed Jane Fonda looks over her shoulder, her blonde hair pinned up in a small bouffant, her lips full and puckered. She's 22 in this spread, fresh off her first screen role in Joshua Logan's *Tall Story*, in which she plays a co-ed shamelessly in pursuit of a husband. Encouraged by Lee Strasberg, her coach at the Actors Studio since 1958, Fonda hungrily pursued a career as an actress in a time when changing sexual mores were trickling into the subtext of popular American cinema. "The American Bardot" reads one of the magazine's headlines, a label that stuck to Fonda years before marrying Roger Vadim, the French director formerly married to the real-life Brigitte Bardot. Despite the comparisons, Hollywood (and later Vadim himself) downplayed Fonda's beauty and sensuality, which supposedly paled in comparison to the French vixen and other blonde bombshells of the time. "I'm no [Marilyn] Monroe. There's no point fooling myself on that score," Fonda said to *Pageant* writer Martha Weinman, "And I'm not a beatnik. I feel fortunate in having a bit of everything, and—this sounds awful—I think I have a certain quality of class."

This "quality of class," which Weinman went on to describe as a compound of "intelligence, dignity, and the faint beginnings of arrogance," was part of the reason young Jane so convincingly embodied the tensions facing women of her generation. With the ascent of second wave feminism and the sexual revolution, young women were caught in limbo between the values of the

---

[78] Beatrice Loayza is a writer and critic based in Washington, D.C.

past and attractive new visions of the future. Fonda's early work unspooled alongside these developments from her very first movie, and in the nearly decade-long period before the antics of *Barbarella* (1968) established Jane as a full-fledged sex icon, her roles in a number of sex comedies and racy dramas embodied the anxiety of American gender politics in transition. What's more, she looked like an ingénue: baby-faced and rail-thin at the time, she didn't pass for a freewheeling sexpot. This, and perhaps the "arrogance" and "dignity" of her pedigree as the daughter of a enormous star made her characters' moral conflicts all the more convincing. "She's not overtly sexy," Logan observed, "but terribly, terribly romantic looking." Like it or not, Jane Fonda at the start of the '60s was a paragon of the mid-century woman's sexual and moral ambivalence.

In *The Chapman Report* (1962), Fonda plays a guilt-ridden young widow, Kathleen, who nervously recalls her strained relationship with her recently deceased pilot husband as evidence of her sexual frigidity. Based on the novel of the same name by Irving Wallace, the film, directed by George Cukor, follows the sexual lives of four women living in the L.A. suburbs of Brentwood: Shelley Winters plays the adulteress, Claire Bloom the psychosexually deranged nympho, Glynis Johns the bored housewife, and Fonda a daddy's girl disinclined to physical intimacy. Sexologist George Chapman (Andrew Duggan) and his assistant Paul Radford (Efrem Zimbalist Jr.) arrive in Brentwood to conduct a sex survey for which these women become case studies. Chapman (who is swarmed upon his arrival by reporters with questions like "Why do women marry?" and "Are men capable of sexual loyalty?") is a riff on Alfred Kinsey and the Kinsey Reports—the studies published in 1948 and 1953 respectively that sparked discussions which began to question rigid understandings of sexuality.

The Kinsey notion that heterosexual women could enjoy sex as much as their male counterparts was particularly suggestive, and it's an idea that *The Chapman Report* encourages so long as these pleasures exist within the bounds of marriage. There's something distasteful (though in keeping with the moment) about a film that so readily buys into feminine stereotypes tailored solely to a woman's unique relationship to men. But the expressions of quivering, frustrated desire manifested by the four central performers register deep tragedy and easy humor in a way that pierces through Cukor and cinematographer Harold Lipstein's clinical visual assemblage, clothing the women in color-coded attire against a melancholy blue backdrop (white for Kathleen, and brown for Bloom's jezebel, for instance). Fonda's character happens to have the most virtuous pathology of the four women; scarred by her emotionally abusive past relationship into believing she completely lacks physical desires, Kathleen pushes back against the notion that her love means less without a robust sexual component.

As the ideas proposed by Kinsey's findings picked up steam throughout the '50s, a number of developments loosened the Production Code Administration's (PCA) grip on Hollywood. These changes fostered the rise of sex comedies featuring bachelor pad titillations and women playing things fast and loose—the sorts of films that defined, in large part, Fonda's screen career up to and including *Barbarella*. One year after the Supreme Court ruled that motion pictures were forms of expression entitled to First Amendment protection, Otto Preminger and United Artists challenged the PCA for the right to incorporate at-the-time provocative verbiage in the script for *The Moon Is Blue* (1953). His film became the first Hollywood film to use the word "virgin" and the first to be released without the PCA's seal of approval; 10 years later the social function of a woman's virginity is at the very heart of *Sunday in New York* (1963), a screwball comedy directed by Peter Tewksbury (the *Father Knows Best* director making his feature debut) and written by Norman Krasna (in the second-to-last screen credit of a career stretching back to the 1930s and including *Mr. and Mrs. Smith*).

As Eileen, a chaste young woman fed up with the toll of her sexual inexperience, Fonda received some of the highest praise in her career thus far, with critics noting her talents as a gifted comedienne. (Years later Pauline Kael described Fonda during this early period as a "charming, witty nudie cutie.") When Eileen arrives at her big brother's apartment in New York City, she bluntly raises the question of whether a girl should go to bed with a man before getting hitched. Beaus keep dumping her, she claims, because of her refusal. Appalled, brother Adam (Cliff Robertson) insists on his heart's honor that this is definitely not the case, even as he himself regularly indulges in a philandering, bachelor lifestyle. But Eileen—thanks to Fonda's candid, spirited presence—is no chump, and her perceived integrity has Adam tiptoeing around his pre-arranged Sunday tryst to conceal from her his own indecency. When she drops the virginity question in her opening monologue, Fonda's voice booms fearlessly, conveying how fed up the character is with the "rules" of sex. For the remaining hour and a half, Fonda's morals are challenged by the hypocrisy of her older brother and complicated by the entry of a charming man (Rod Taylor) she meets on a Fifth Avenue bus.

Three years later, Fonda graduated from frustrated virgin into reluctant mistress in Robert Ellis Miller's debut film *Any Wednesday* (1966), which has Fonda's sprightly Ellen seduced (not through the temptation of sex, mind you, but through a paid-for apartment and room full of balloons) by a wealthy, married business executive, John (Jason Robards). Initially Ellen rebuffs John's advances, but appalled as she may be by his audacity in spite of his wife and kids back home, his sensitivity, persistence, and willingness to indulge her whims eventually lead to her capitulation. Like Eileen in *Sunday in New York*, Ellen is baffled and worn out by the intrepidly horny men around her, a predicament that allows Fonda to make excellent use of her maximalist performing tendencies: after her lover's wife, for instance, suddenly appears at her secret apartment, Fonda confronts the man with screams and charged physicality. At the same time, Fonda plays a glamorous version of the modern New York woman so naturally—whether confessing to her fiancé her near-sexual tryst while the two slow-dance at a glitzy nightclub in *Sunday in New York*, or as a kept woman in *Any Wednesday* strutting around her Manhattan condo provided by her lover in a sheer negligee with comically long sleeves. Moral fortitude notwithstanding, the faint glimmers of Bree Daniels, Fonda's anguished sex worker character in *Klute* (1971), are already perceptible.

All Steadicam and No Play: Movement in *The Shining*

by Anya Stanley[79]

In 1998, Stanley Kubrick accepted the D.W. Griffith Award from the Director's Guild of America. In his acceptance speech, he compared Griffith to the Grecian myth of Icarus. Like Icarus, Griffith flew too close to the sun, but instead of his wax-and-feather wings melting, Griffith was shunned by the movie industry he largely created. Did Kubrick take this as the cautionary tale that it's been accepted as for millennia, to avoid flying too high? No; instead, he recognized it as a call to "do a better job on the wings."

As we celebrate the 40th anniversary of Kubrick's horror film *The Shining*, social media and video retrospectives will be brimming with now-classic images: a boy turning corner after corner on his tricycle, a man with an axe limping like a wounded beast through a serpentine hedge maze. None of these images would be as memorable in the cultural consciousness were it not for Kubrick's gamble on "better wings," in the form of Garrett Brown's Steadicam technology.

In an episode of YouTube series *The Science of Movies*, Brown explains that he simply engineered a product that was missing in filmmaking at the time. "Cameras had to be on wheels to make a smooth moving shot. When I first got in the business, I had to buy a huge dolly to put my stupid little camera on. People go places where you couldn't use a dolly. Dramas take place across doorsteps, and up steps. Over rough ground you can use a dolly and lay rails, but you can't look ahead, you can't look behind.

---

[79] Anya Stanley is a Fangoria Magazine columnist, a Rotten Tomatoes-approved film critic, and staunch Halloween 6 apologist. Her work at various bylines (including Collider, The AV Club, and Crooked Marquee) can be found at her website www.anyawrites.com.

That's crazy; it just seemed, to me, so restrictive." He relocated the camera's center of gravity to an external point below it, placing a stabilizing gimbal and counterweights behind and underneath the camera, connecting it to the operator's harness via an articulated arm. The effect is that the camera can feel free-floating while being handheld, untainted by operator movement. His 1974 demo video (widely available on YouTube)[80] includes, among other things, his then-girlfriend Ellen running along a hillside. The camera effortlessly glides alongside her like a child following a sea lion along an aquarium display. The reel made the rounds in the film industry, landing Brown three feature film projects the following year: John Avildsen's *Rocky*, Hal Ashby's *Bound for Glory*, and John Schlesinger's *Marathon Man*. Eventually, the game-changing tech caught the eye of a game-changing auteur, and in 1979, Garrett Brown was hired to film a haunted house picture.

Vincent LoBrutto's Stanley Kubrick biography (of the same title) details how Brown got attached to *The Shining*. A film exhibition in London drew the director's interest just as the Stephen King adaptation entered pre-production, and Kubrick hosted a sit-down with Brown at his Boreham Wood home, where they showed him the latest evolution of the Steadicam design. According to LoBrutto, Kubrick asked Brown to demonstrate the accuracy he could achieve with the Steadicam, having him hit marks in order to pull focus when working at the high exposures he would require during shooting. Kubrick thought several steps ahead and ensured that the technology he worked with allowed for the movement and precision that he envisioned for telling the story.

On his audio commentary for the 2007 Blu-ray release of the

---

[80] Time, First, Its, Has, Everything, "The first Steadicam Test Shots, by Garrett Brown, the inventor, 1974," YouTube (September 18, 2019) https://www.youtube.com/watch?v=M1Gt51hvBm0&feature=youtu.be.

film, Brown credits the filmmaker for foreseeing the ways that the on screen image could be manipulated with his invention. "I think I had perhaps done 8 other movies before *The Shining*," he comments. "I tended to do special shots, brought in to do this or that sequence; it didn't occur to people– until Stanley got the idea– that this was a tool that you could use every day, I felt. This was the first time that I was there for the entire schedule, beginning to end, and available as Stanley's tool or weapon for penetrating space, for following things without laying rails or worrying about the quality of the ground."

A Gothic tale enmeshed in modern geometric interiors, The Shining is a pageant of madness that presents a family in its spotlight. Jack Torrance (Jack Nicholson), an author with anger issues and substance abuse in his history, is hired as the caretaker of the Overlook Hotel during its long, harsh winter. He brings along his family: mousy wife Wendy (Shelley Duvall) and son Danny (Danny Lloyd), who has a special gift that allows him to see things most people can't. In the snow-blanketed isolation of the Rocky mountains, cut off from roads and rescue, the trio slowly learn that something is dreadfully wrong with their seasonal dwelling.

As he did with sci-fi (in 1968's *2001: A Space Odyssey*), Kubrick avoided the conventional elements of a genre picture. You're not going to see Jack Torrance illuminated in uncanny facial lighting from below, like so many camp counselors shining a flashlight under their chins as they tell ghost stories. Instead, Kubrick shot in existing, meticulous light, obsessively concerned with composition. As an avid chess player, he was intimately aware of spatial awareness, discerning how things and people related to their surroundings. This glistens through the entire 146-minute runtime; the compositions are direct, center-framed and delicately staged. The result is enchanting: as the family descends into hysteria, the audience descends, getting lost in the labyrinthine recesses of the characters' minds. In the featurette *The Visions of Stanley*

Kubrick, cinematographer Janusz Kamiński (a regular collaborator with Steven Spielberg) talks about the medium's power to pull an audience in: "Filmmakers always look for ways to allow the audience to participate in the movie. One of the ways you allow them to be active participants is with a mobile camera."

With *The Shining*, movement is the name of the game. With the work of cinematographer John Alcott, Kubrick uses the kinetic gaze of the camera to act as another character in the story, prowling along corridors and craning its neck around the doors of forbidden rooms. He mostly filmed in an aspect ratio of 1.66:1, which nestled the look of the film glamorously, something between widescreen and CinemaScope. With that, the frame is filled, and the viewer has no choice but to stare down the madness unfolding before them. Even when the characters are immobile, the camera provides the movement. Crawling zooms uncover information about them, such as Jack losing his mind as he stares out a window, or Dick Halloran's "shine" as he lays in bed. A long lens softly blurs everything else around Jack while emphasizing his advancement towards Wendy, making the monster even more monstrous. But among all of these techniques, the combination of wide lenses and Brown's Steadicam do the most to capitalize on the sense of hypnotic movement in the film. From the grand tour of the hotel to the mesmerizing, ice-cold climax, Steadicam allows the viewer to penetrate the onscreen space, into the story itself.

There was a lot to navigate within that space. The shooting sets were massive, the result of Kubrick's insistence upon most of the interiors being built to scale. If there is action, Garrett Brown shot it. "I actually shot almost all the moving shots in that film," Brown told CBS Sunday Morning[81] "All the stuff in the corridors. (Kubrick) had in his mind this eerie smoothness. And that, we were able to deliver. That almost turned it into the hotel's point of

---

[81] Morning, Sunday, CBS, "How the Steadicam changed movies," YouTube (March 4, 2018) https://www.youtube.com/watch?v=vF4jPaFQNHo.

view." The only two major sequences of movement that Brown didn't lens were the opening helicopter shot of the Torrance family driving through the mountains, and the high-tension moment when Wendy discovers Jack's manuscript and is confronted by him. Both were done by the second unit crew and a Steadicam understudy, Ray Andrew. For the rest—the hedge maze, the tricycle run, the ballroom—Brown was there, armed with a BL Silent 35mm camera.

Though he had invented the apparatus, Brown honed his craft on the set of *The Shining*. His first challenge came during the scene between Danny's doctor and Wendy at the Torrance home, just after we meet Danny's imaginary friend Tony for the first time; it's a simple enough tracking shot, but Brown was required to hold his rig perfectly still at the end of it for several minutes at a time while the actors completed the scene, essentially acting as a tripod impersonator. The trick is to check the periphery of the frame in the sequence after any tracking shot: if there's a bit of movement in the corners, that's Brown bearing the 60 pound rig as if it's a crane arm for two, sometimes three minutes. Anyone who has held a body plank for thirty seconds has a fair idea of the kind of core strength one would need for such a feat, and Brown was put through such practices over and over throughout the shooting schedule. On his audio commentary, he recalls the benefit of Kubrick's infamous precision. "We were on the set for four days, and I then shot 30 or 40 times. Then I realized that the essence of it had almost nothing to do with me, because my takes were roughly identical. It had to do with Stanley watching and watching, and waiting, and letting the performance play up or play down. I liked participating in that way of working, because I got a chance to refine what I did to an extent that I never did before, like a dancer rehearsing, or being onstage every night for a year. I got to learn the closest dimensions of the apartment and what would happen if this foot was six inches in this direction, or if I took another half step."

It wasn't always physically demanding; sometimes the immense geography of the interiors were too much to navigate by foot. Brown tried multiple vehicles so that he wouldn't have to walk with the Steadicam for the tracking shots, including arguably the most iconic, following young Danny as he takes his bike for a joyride throughout the corridors. After some pushback, the director himself (along with Ron Ford) created a specialized wheelchair so that Brown could operate his camera with a focus on framing, rather than pacing as he tried to keep up. Steadicam rickshaws are widely utilized in filmmaking now, but in 1980, it was just another day of troubleshooting on the set.

In order to follow Danny Lloyd around, Brown couldn't hold the camera at the usual level. Tilting downward towards the boy while filming in the wide-angled lenses that Kubrick loved so much would result in "keystoning," in which the lenses would distort the image too much, giving it a bizarre funhouse mirror look. So, more innovation was needed. Brown crafted an upside-down version of the Steadicam with the camera on the bottom and the rest of it on top. This way, the lens would be in what Brown calls "low mode," between waist and knee. This allowed the camera to stay level from front to rear, and eliminated lens tilting. The low mode was used most effectively in the scenes that featured Danny riding on his tricycle throughout the hotel. With the lens mere inches above the floor, the viewfinder (and thus the audience) can infiltrate the screen territory right behind the child. The operator doesn't have to make wide arcs around corners as they would have to on a dolly; they can stay with the actor and cut those corners for fluidity. The more fluidity, the more the image resembles what the actual human eye registers while moving throughout a space. Slip an ultra-wide lens over it and that child's vehicle, bouncing throughout the convolutions of a hotel, begins to take on the appearance of people rattling around within a giant indoor maze.

The flow of the camera movement pays off the most in the hedge maze sequence at the film's end. The cheese has fully slid off of Jack Torrance's cracker, and he attacks his family. Wendy and Danny are split up, the boy enters the hedge maze beside the hotel, and his maniacal father follows him, axe in hand. In following Danny and Jack, Brown moves as fluidly as the blood pours from the elevators. He explains the waltz between actor and operator thus: "This was actually a handheld shot of mine. So here is that 9.8 mm lens, held dead-level. Pushing through space, revealing god knows what. There was no way to plan any of it; Jack went somewhere, and I reacted. This is done in the 'Don Juan' mode of Steadicam, when you run forward, but you're shooting backwards. This is almost a dance, totally ad-libbed, not the same twice. Stanley off somewhere, watching on wireless video, shouting in comments sometimes by walkie-talkie, acting like some sort of wrathful Nielsen Family, watching, judging, controlling the content." The payload is a mesmerizing visual of terror that imprints upon the psyche. A wide lens with the unrelenting Steadicam movement gives everything within its eye an exaggerated appearance. The hedges, originally greenery nailed to slabs of plywood, built on a London airfield, now threaten to swallow its trespassers whole. The spatial relations of actor to setting change, taking on a sinister air within the crosshairs of the viewfinder. This is the power of mobile filmmaking.

Stanley Kubrick is rightfully credited with changing the language of cinema, but Garrett Brown and his Steadicam made a meaningful contribution to the vocabulary Kubrick used to do so. For his part, Brown recognizes the role that the film played in his career. "I think I learned my trade on The Shining, really," he comments. "I was good with the thing when I showed up; I think I can say without modesty that I became an absolute master of it by the end of this schedule, through the miracle of repetition." He went on to invent several devices that allow a viewer to follow a subject through spaces previously un-navigable for home viewers. The Steadicam utilizes the most dynamic form of the medium: to draw the audience into a world they might not otherwise access. Steven Spielberg once said that it's impossible to turn off a Kubrick film; Brown's wandering eye is one reason why.

Black Panther Raises Big Questions about Identity and Loyalty
by Doc Ayomide[82]

Black Panther confronted me with two big questions I find simultaneously longstanding and fresh.

"#BlackPanther effectively asks one big question, and then uses characters to embody several derivative sub-questions in a way that layers its tensions (and makes Civil War, good as that was, almost one-dimensional by comparison). And that's just one aspect of its genius." – @DocAyomide, Feb 16, 2018.

The best stories are those that continue long after the last page has turned or credits have rolled. But even among these best, there are two sub-categories.

There are those that have produced fundamental shifts in how I see things—single stories like Thomas Hardy's *Tess of the D'Urbervilles* and Ursula K Le Guin's *The Wizard of Earthsea*, and The Matrix (the first one, thank you), and epic sagas like JRR Tolkien's *The Lord of the Rings* (the books and movies alike) and the grand story of my Christian faith, among others. These are the great stories of my life, each representing one or more major landmarks in my emotional and moral maturity.

And then there are what I think of as the really good stories: the ones that raise serious questions about how I see things. Where

---

[82] Doc Ayomide is a writer and psychiatrist specialist training in psychiatry. He has spent over a decade thinking, writing and speaking about what it means to be human from various angles, including behavioural psychology, faith and storytelling. He has featured on various Nigerian radio and TV stations, on international media including HuffPost, and invited to speak several events, including TEDx. He loves a good debate and now lives and practises in UK. You can say hello to him on Twitter or email him: hello@docayomide.com.

the first kind make bold statements, these kinds pose challenges without necesarily claiming to offer answers. It is in this latter sub-category that Black Panther falls.

I knew after the first time I saw it that I wanted to see it again, but I wanted to give it some time to percolate first. So I wrote down (and tweeted some of) my initial thoughts, checked out think pieces and reviews, talked about it with others who'd seen it, and all of that engagement with other perspectives and positions deepened my understanding of the questions on my second viewing.

Black Panther raises the two big questions of identity and loyalty: 1) Who are you?; and 2) What are you loyal to?

Big question #1: Who are you?

I noticed this question from the first time but it wasn't until my second viewing that I realised how deeply embedded in the story it is. But let's consider it through the lenses of the three key instances of the question.

Opening Scene

The question comes in a triple sequence here. First N'Jobu asks who is at the door (this is where Zuri responds with the now well-known quip about "Grace Jones-looking ladies," and N'Jobu warns that they won't knock a second time). Then T'Chaka asks N'Jobu to identify himself as a Wakandan (which he does to Zuri's apparent surprise). Then he asks Zuri to identify himself as a Wakandan spy, to N'Jobu's true surprise.

This kind of triple sequence is used in story to, as I understand it, show a connection, strengthen the connection and then subvert the connection. Right from the start of the story, it is used effectively in foreshadowing the importance of identity to this story, with the question of who one is being used thrice to reveal surprises: the first two times with a tension that is relieved (by the Grace Jones joke in the first and by delight of a father in the second), and the third time subverting by revealing the surprise of betrayal.

Branded Content Pivotal Mid-Story Scene

Killmonger faces down T'Challa and the Wakandan leadership and taunts them into challenging his identity and the elder shouts, "Who are you?" Like in the first instance of the identity question, this second instance is also about surprise, but not to us as the audience, because this time we feel like we're in on it: we, like T'Challa, know who Killmonger is, and surprise is on the Wakandan leadership. But it turns out there is a surprise in store for us too, for as we soon discover, we don't fully grasp the implications of our inside knowledge: Killmonger's true identity grants him an unexpected legitimacy. Once again, unknown identity underlies betrayal. The second instance strengthens the connection.

Closing Scene

Here the question comes from a boy who, unlike his mates, is less fascinated by what T'Challa and Shuri have, as much as he is by who they are. "Who are you?" he asks, smiling, and we smile with him, because this time we are fully in on it and there are no surprises. We know his life is about to change for the better, and perhaps for good.

Where the first two instances of the identity question set us up for a surprise that proves unpleasant, this one subverts the connection by setting up a surprise that we can enjoy. And this time we really are in on it. (This theme of a surprise we are in on is echoed in the first after-credits scene, which is why I get the criticism about the scene being somewhat redundant.)

And this doesn't even cover all the times identity comes up in the story. There's when T'Challa's mother Ramonda yells at him to remember who he is during the first fight against M'Baku. There's the reminder from T'Chaka too. And there's the questions about who Agent Ross is.

So there's no doubt to me that a big question that what the story is intended to raise is about identity. Who are you? Do you know where you come from? Do you know what you represent, what you stand for, to whom you belong? And do you grasp the multifaceted implications of your identity? And underlying all that is the sense that to not know all this is to set yourself up for possible disappointment when it matters most.

Big question #2: What are you most loyal to?

But the identity question is tightly related to the loyalty question: one of the implications of who you are is what you are going to be loyal to.

Here's what I tweeted about Okoye after seeing the movie the first time. Someone had just tweeted about Okoye putting her country first always in response to a question by Kelechnekoff about whether Okoye was Machiavellian, but I didn't feel like that characterisation captured her with quite enough nuance:

"Not at all, she puts her country above herself always." (replying to @kelechnekoff) Feb 18, 2018.

"I feel like her loyalty wasn't to nation as much as to throne. Her character arc was basically her redefining her loyalty to the throne: at first to THRONE IN ITSELF (even if it destroyed the nation) and then to THRONE AS SYMBOL for the nation (permitting her to challenge it).

I loved that because that's really all of us. So many things we see as one until they separate and then we're forced to rethink how they're dif-

ferent without losing how they're connected—and how tightly." —Doc Ayomide, Feb 18, 2018.

Exploring the complexity of what Okoye's arc and what it means for us would require a whole other article (which I may well write) but the point here is that she stands as great example of someone who, while maintaining her loyalty (it didn't exactly change over the course of the story), had to redefine what exactly that loyalty meant. And that's a reality we all face in real life.

But Okoye was not the only character who had to redefine what loyalty meant to her. Nobody, in fact, embodies the two questions of loyalty and identity like T'Challa himself. To illustrate this, allow me to share yet another tweet from my first-viewing thoughts:

"Several ways to define the big #BlackPanther question, but I'd articulate it (for now) as, "When I have to choose, what do I most owe loyalty to?" My lover? My ethnic group? My nation? My race? Humanity? The past? (See who represents which?) Pretty keen to write on this." —@Docayomide, Feb 16 2018.

Here's the thing: while other characters prioritise their chosen loyalty almost exclusively, T'Challa is the one character who seeks to embody all the loyalties in a sort of equilibrium. Where other characters quickly abandon other loyalties in favour of their preferred one, he seeks to maintain each of his loyalties without abandoning the others. And the ongoing tension from this balancing act is perhaps borne out in a fact I've heard several comments on: he seems rather understated—overshadowed, even—in his own movie.

Where Letitia Wright wins hearts everywhere with her characterisation of Shuri as a playful genius and Danai Gurira impresses with her portrayal of Okoye as a general with a sense of dignity matched only by her quietly sardonic humour, Chadwick

Boseman's T'Challa is a stoic soul who smiles seldom, and never (as I recall) at his own joke. Even Andy Serkis' Ulysses Klaue has a wild sense of sociopathic humour, and Michael B Jordan's Killmonger (who admittedly also seldom smiles) certainly makes up for his own lack of humour with a passionate anger that ever simmers just beneath the surface.

T'Challa, however, is serious. And while this has (understandably) bothered some people, I find it to fit the fact that he, of all the characters, struggles most with reconciling all the tensions the others pick and choose from. Again and again, T'Challa refuses to pick and choose. He is not fond of the either-or, but a man of the both-and.

We see this play out, when, immediately he assumes the throne, an elder pointedly tells him the nation needs a king and not a warrior, and while he does not respond, it is clear he believes they can have both, instead of one or the other.

T'Challa is not a man of extremes and passion, but a man of restraint and balance who, even as a warrior will not take a life if he can avoid it (a character trait established from his appearance in Civil War), which is why his father astutely observes, "You are a good man, with a good heart, and it is hard for a good man to be king." And that is another tension he seeks to resolve: being a good man and a good king, not one or the other.

And even in the end, even after he yells at his ancestors that they were all wrong, it is not in order to simply dispose of the legacies of the past, but to admit its liabilities as well, and to reconcile the past with the present, instead of simply ignoring the present in favour of the past.

So what is T'Challa loyal to? In the end, it is, I think, to truth.

And it is this loyalty to truth that differentiates him from the kind of fickle person who has no loyalties. Because he's not loyal to nothing. Actually not even the fickle person is loyal to nothing: they are loyal to themselves, to their egos. But not so T'Challa. He is not a man without loyalties, but a man with a higher loyalty by which he seeks to order all his other loyalties. He is loyal to what is right and true, and he refuses (unlike Okoye, who is incidentally my favourite character) to settle for easy answers as to what that means.

That's the kind of person I want to be.

The Beautiful Girls: The Dynamic Women of *Mad Men*

by Angela Morrison[83]

Mad Men's seven seasons trace the lives of its characters as they navigate the tumultuous 1960s in New York City, each of them facing romantic, professional, and personal struggles that are only compounded[84] by the violence and upheaval that defined American culture and politics at this time. *Mad Men*'s attention to detail in recreating the stylish 60s is remarkable, with its warm cinematography, expertly-selected pop music cues, cultural references from Ritz crackers to I Am Curious (Yellow), and, of course, the meticulously crafted fashion, makeup, and hairstyles.

What makes this attention to detail all the more impressive is the fact that the show keeps up with the rapidly changing artistic, cultural, political, and sartorial landscapes of the 60s as its seasons progress. Tailored black-and-white suits and slicked-back hair give way to moustaches and suede, and dresses are traded in for brightly coloured blouses and pants. Long-form television is the perfect medium for capturing the subtle (and sometimes not-so-subtle)[85] changes that occur in people's lives over a period of many years. *Mad Men*'s manifold group of female characters face some of the most drastic, messy, complicated upheavals in the series, and the way that the show builds these women's lives deserves more critical attention.

---

[83] Angela Morrison is a freelance pop culture writer and PhD student in Cinema and Media Studies at the University of British Columbia. Her research is focused on the intersections between melodrama, camp, and queer theory in television series such as RuPaul's Drag Race and films by John Waters and Anna Biller. She lives in Toronto and can most likely be found drinking coffee and discussing the cultural importance of Mariah Carey.
[84] Docterman, Eliana, "History as Seen on Mad Men: A Timeline," *TIME* (May 18, 2015) https://time.com/3858844/mad-men-historical-events/.
[85] Etkin, Jaimie, "We Need To Talk About Those Epic Mustaches On "Mad Men"," *BuzzFeed* (April 5, 2015) https://www.buzzfeed.com/jaimieetkin/who-has-the-best-70s-mustache-on-mad-men.

This time period in America is characterized by violent assassinations, the Vietnam War, hippie culture, and social movements against racism, homophobia, and sexism (notably through the rise of second-wave feminism). As Rachel Catlett writes: "The characters are not necessarily feminists, but *Mad Men*, at its core, is a series primarily concerned with the struggles of women in the 60s."[86] The show does not always explicitly reference second-wave feminism and "women's liberation," but, over the course of the series, the characters confront violence and dismissal based on their gender, some of which inspires them to fight back and reject the limitations placed upon them. Caroline Framke astutely points out that *Mad Men* is a show populated by men who want to change but cannot, and women who demonstrate remarkably rich inner lives and the ability to grow and change in ways the men would never even dream of.[87]

The show most closely follows Peggy Olson (Elisabeth Moss), who begins the series as a shy, awkward secretary and ends it as a confident, self-assured businesswoman, a badass creative force to be reckoned with. In the first season's "Babylon," Peggy participates in a brainstorming session for Belle Jolie lipstick, and her creative turns of phrase ("a basket of kisses") catch the attention of her older male colleague, Freddy Rumsen (Joel Murray), who then asks her to write copy for the company's advertisements. Thus begins Peggy's rise up the corporate ladder at Sterling Cooper (and later, Cutler, Gleason & Chaough), and, although she is consistently patronized by her male colleagues and clients and underappreciated by her boss, Don Draper (Jon Hamm), she refuses to give up because she knows that she is good at her job and deserves her position on the creative team.

Peggy's professional triumphs often seem to come at a price, and she frequently finds herself in the uncomfortable position of

---

[86] Catlett, Rachel, "An Ode to the Feminism of Mad Men," *The Mary Sue* (May 26, 2015) https://www.themarysue.com/ode-to-feminism-of-mad-men/.

[87] Framke, Caroline, "10 years ago, Mad Men began a story of men who tried to change — and the women who actually did," *Vox* (July 19, 2017) https://www.vox.com/culture/2017/7/19/15992342/mad-men-anniversary-don-peggy-joan.

feeling as though she has to choose between her career and personal/romantic fulfillment. In the first season, Peggy has a brief affair with the newly-married Pete Campbell (Vincent Kartheiser) and accidentally becomes pregnant, a fact that she keeps secret from almost everyone, save for Don, her family, and eventually Pete. Peggy makes the conscious decision not to keep her baby, demonstrating remarkable strength in the face of this life-altering decision. Rather than follow the traditional path expected of women in the 60s of finding a man, getting married, and settling down to start a family, Peggy opts to spend almost all of her time at the office, finding herself alone in the empty building on weekends, holidays, and late at night. The few people she ends up dating, Mark (Blake Bashoff) and Abe (Charlie Hofheimer), end up resenting her for being distant and more committed to her work than to their relationships.

Peggy's transformation from a timid, inexperienced young woman to a brash, badass lead copywriter is never clearer than in the seventh season's "Lost Horizon," when she arrives at the new Sterling Cooper & Partners offices swaggering down the hallway in dark sunglasses, cigarette hanging out of her mouth, proudly carrying the painting she inherited from Bert Cooper, The Dream of the Fisherman's Wife.[88] The advertising world is rife with toxic masculinity, and while Peggy resents constantly being subjected to sexist remarks and behaviour, she also takes inspiration from the assertive, overly confident men she works with. Peggy sees men get away with terrible behaviour and over time decides that she, too, should be allowed to do so. She makes her opinion known, no matter the consequences, as in the fifth season premiere, "A Little Kiss," when she looks the Heinz executives in the eye and fights for her "Bean Ballet" advertisement, arguing that her pitch is fresh and beautiful, terms rarely associated with baked beans.

---

[88] "The Dream of the Fisherman's Wife," Wikipedia
https://en.wikipedia.org/wiki/The_Dream_of_the_Fisherman%27s_Wife.

Peggy is not always kind, and does not always make the best decisions ("I stabbed Abe…"), but she learns a lot about herself over the course of the series, and learns to navigate her difficult position as a professional woman in a patriarchal society. Perhaps nobody else besides Peggy knows the deep struggle of being a working woman more than Joan Holloway (Christina Hendricks), Sterling Cooper's head secretary and later one of the firm's partners. When Peggy first arrives at Sterling Cooper, the voluptuous, confident Joan advises her on how to present herself and how to talk to men. Over the years, Joan and Peggy's relationship becomes fraught at times as they try to help each other navigate the sometimes violently sexist industry in which they work.

Even as Joan acquires more respect and authority, her colleagues (men and women both) see her as nothing more than a sexual object. She is often good-natured when clients comment on her beauty and her body, but over time becomes worn out and angry. By the time she tells Peggy, "I want to burn this place to the ground," after being sexually harassed in a meeting, it is clear that Joan will no longer tolerate being diminished and not taken seriously. Christina Hendricks beautifully portrays how Joan's hurt, anger, and humiliation grow and deepen over time, pain caused by being raped by her husband, Greg (Samuel Page), being pressured by her male colleagues into having sex with a Jaguar executive in exchange for being made partner, and discovering her dear friend Lane Pryce's (Jared Harris) dead body after he commits suicide. What makes Hendricks's performance so brilliant is the way that Joan sometimes allows her tough exterior to crack, as when she throws a model airplane at Meredith (Stephanie Drake) or confronts Lane and remarks that she has yet to meet a man who does not treat her like a "helpless, stupid little girl."

By the seventh season, Joan grows to realize that the only person she can rely on is herself, everyone else be damned. She and Greg divorce and she decides to raise her baby on her own, with little involvement from his biological father, Roger Sterling (John Slattery). After years of workplace harassment and mistreatment, Joan decides to start her own film production company that will be run out of her living room, an ambitious move that prompts her boyfriend, Richard (Bruce Greenwood), to leave her. Joan was always mature, disciplined, and brave, but she finally blossoms toward the end of the series as she begins to trust in her own talents more than she ever had before. Joan faced profound difficulties during the 1960s, yet the series suggests that the 1970 offers the dawning of a new and brighter era for her.

Betty Francis (January Jones) is perhaps the character with the most tragic ending. At times cold, uncaring, and vicious, Betty spends most of the series in misery. Yet Betty is compelling in the way she can be mean one moment and incredibly sensitive the next. She loves her children fiercely, but the way she shows affection sometimes looks and feels like rage. Betty begins the series as a perfectly-manicured docile housewife, speaking in a soft voice and capitulating to Don's every desire, perhaps willfully ignoring his shady behaviour. It is not until the second season's "A Night to Remember" that Betty truly crumbles after Don's colleagues poke fun at her during dinner, after which she spends a number of days wearing the same dress and drinking red wine in bed. After this, Betty makes the wise decision to leave Don, and begins the process of becoming more assertive (some would argue too assertive).

By the time Betty receives a fatal diagnosis of lung cancer, she has caused considerable damage in a number of her relationships: with Don, with Sally (Kiernan Shipka), and with her second husband, Henry Francis (Christopher Stanley). Her diagnosis is particularly tragic as it comes in the midst of her pursuing a psychology degree, a huge step for perpetual housewife Betty. After a number of unhappy relationships and unfulfilling years at home, Betty finally sees more for herself and her future, and going back to school is one of the few decisions that she makes solely for her own benefit. Despite her chilly exterior, she spends much of the series thinking about her children and her husband(s), doing what she can to provide them with good, comfortable lives (although not always in the most conventional ways). Toward the end of the series, she takes a step back and acknowledges her own intelligence—as she says to Henry, "I'm not stupid, you know. I can speak Italian!" Her stubbornness prevails as she refuses treatment and gives her family instructions on what to do in the event of her death.

The last glimpse we get of Betty—in "Person to Person"—finds her seated at her kitchen table smoking a cigarette while Sally washes the dishes. This scene heartbreakingly suggests that Sally will be the one taking on the housework after her mother is gone, a loss likely to happen in the near future. The other undercurrent of the scene is the fact that Sally and Betty have finally mended some of their resentment toward each other, a reconciliation catalyzed by the most unfortunate circumstances.

Sally experiences some of the most drastic changes of any character in the series. The first time we see her, she is a tiny munchkin, running around the house making trouble with Bobby (Maxwell Huckabee, later replaced by a number of different actors). Over time, Sally witnesses more debauchery and emotionally volatile situations than any little girl should ever have to. Her resentment toward both of her parents builds over time, as her mother becomes more spiteful and her father more pathetic, lost, and broken. Sally grows up quickly as a result, enduring her parents' divorce, her grandfather's death, and both Don and Betty's remarriages before she even turns fifteen.

Sally's curiosity sometimes gets her into trouble, as when she gets caught smoking a cigarette in the closet or masturbating at her friend's house during a sleepover. Kiernan Shipka displays remarkable maturity in her characterization of Sally, and has a particular knack for delivering lines with blunt sincerity. Who can forget the ending of "At the Codfish Ball," when Sally, having accidentally walked in on Marie (Julia Ormond) going down on Roger, bluntly proclaims that New York is "dirty," or when she coldly tells Betty, cigarette in hand,

"My father has never given me anything," after she sees him cheating on Megan with his neighbour, Sylvia Rosen (Linda Cardellini). Despite Betty's worries that Sally is a perpetual problem child, by the end of the seventh season she has become an intelligent and sensitive young woman who will undoubtedly take wonderful care of her siblings when Betty is gone.

Mad Men undoubtedly made space for women characters to grow, learn, and face personal hardships, some of which have larger political and social resonance. Yet the show never made the same space for its non-white, non-heterosexual women, of which there are only a few. It certainly addresses racism and homophobia at times, yet never in a sustained way, and often only to reveal character development in the straight, white protagonists. In "Mystery Date," Peggy brings secretary Dawn Chambers (Teyonah Parris) to her apartment so that she can stay the night, after Dawn reveals that she's too scared to go home because of violent riots in Harlem. The scene largely focuses on Peggy's awkward attempts at kindness, yet we never get to see how the interaction affects Dawn.

Dawn is one of the only recurring Black characters on the show, but she only appears in scenes taking place at work. Her banter with Peggy's secretary, Shirley (Sola Bamis), is fantastic, but the show's focus on their friendship is only cursory. Dawn is later promoted to head secretary, a monumental move for the closed-minded Sterling Cooper & Partners, but this promotion occurs toward the end of the series, leaving very little room for Dawn to become a protagonist.

Similarly, Peggy's queer friend, Joyce (Zosia Mamet), is never afforded much interiority. She appears sporadically, looking cool in her tailored suits, offering Peggy opportunities to experience art and culture. She takes Peggy to a party/experimental film screening where she first meets Abe, and later shows the creative team at SC&P photos from the Richard Speck murders. Based on these small exchanges, we know very little about Joyce. She is Peggy's cool friend, her gay friend, her photographer friend, yet we never see her again after the fifth season.

Outlining these blind spots serves only to suggest how *Mad Men* could have been more inclusive, and more attuned to the wide variety of people who lived and worked and loved in New York City in the 1960s. *Mad Men* provided television some of its most interesting, complex women for many years, and while the show's anchor is ostensibly Don Draper, the women took it to a beautiful, tragic, angry, brilliant new level.

Everything Daniel Kaluuya Revealed On The Set of *Queen & Slim*
by Jerry Barrow[89]

Daniel's Slim has been tethered to Jodie Turner-Smith's Queen as they make their way across the country in search of freedom, and themselves, after killing a police officer in self-defense.

Daniel Kaluuya is trying to watch his figure. It's about two-thirds into shooting *Queen & Slim*, Lena Waithe's and Melina Matsoukas' ambitious first feature film, and it's a hot Louisiana day in February, right before Mardis Gras. A sheet of icing-filled King Cake is being passed around to the cast and crew, but Kaluuya declines. His costar Braylen Brian Banks ribs him for not partaking in the traditional 'Nawlins dessert, but he may still be working off the calories from the birthday cake he was surprised with a few weeks ago while they were filming in the polar vortex of Ohio.

The sun is setting on the current shoot location, Vic's Auto Glass, a few blocks from McCue Playground Park. Daniel is getting his mic taped to his ankle in preparation for the next shot. It's scene 52, take three, and our heroes are in dire need of assistance on their journey. Daniel's Slim has been tethered to Jodie Turner-Smith's Queen as they make their way across the country in search of freedom, and themselves, after killing a police officer in self-defense.

As characters go, Kaluuya's Slim is the midpoint between his naïve and trusting Chris Washington from *Get Out* and the ruthless killer Jatemme Manning from *Widows*. All three men

---

[89] Jerry Barrow is a writer, creator, and film critic formerly with BET. He is the former editor-in-chief of Scratch Magazine. He is the creator of the creator and host of the Fathers Who Bother Podcast.

end up spilling blood, but for different reasons. In her directorial debut, Melina Matsoukas braids the personalities of both Kaluuya and Turner together in overlapping ways, maintaining their individuality but keeping them inextricably bonded. Slim starts out as an inquisitive, family-oriented young man with a heart who rubs up against Queen's self-imposed analytical solitude. But by the end of the film, they both are transformed physically, emotionally and politically.

Seeking shelter in his trailer from a sudden downpour, Daniel communes with a group of lucky writers to lay out his role in a love story tailor-made for this age.

Why He Took the Part

"The script. It's crazy. I read the script. Lena came to a Get Out screening. That's where I first met her, before Get Out came out. I had read the pilot for The Chi, and I told her she was an incredible writer. Then she mentioned the Bonnie and Clyde story and I said, "What's that?" And then she sent it to me. I went to Comic Con and then on the way back I read it and emailed her and said I want to play Slim. He just feels like an everyman, a guy that wants to do good, but things happen. Standing up for yourself is a dangerous sport at times."

What It's Like Working with Jodie

"She's cool as sh*t. Very fabulous. She's amazing and so smart and so on it. And really open and really supportive. This is a tough shoot and a very tough schedule. I'm really privileged to have her there to kind of like bounce off and spend some time outside of it so we're best prepared."

How His Personal Experience Informs Slim

"I've lived a lot of shit. That's why it spoke to me, man. I've been through a lot in situations with the police. I'm trying not to mess up my career. A lot of my friends can't even get into the country because of saying yes to a [thing] they shouldn't have said yes to at 14 or 15. I understood that.

When we did the opening scene in Cleveland, it was really triggering for me. It really kind of messed me up. It's dark. Being in that space… we're so desensitized to that imagery of being beaten up by the police. It's intimate to me. It's not something that I learned."

Slim's Motivation

"Survival. I empathize with that. Say, someone like Jateme, get it. I get how you get there. If you're in a context that's passively oppressive, you have to do something or you get beat up mentally. That kind of survival, wanting to keep going, to figure stuff out and trying to have a life, I do empathize with that. I see that a lot with my friends."

Working with First-Time Directors: Melina Matsoukas vs. Jordan Peele

"They're very different animals, Melina and Jordan. Jordan is comedy and sketch shows, X, Y, Z. But I was a fan of both of them. I found them both organically. Key and Peele sketches were a thing in my life in my WhatsApp Groups. I remember seeing the "Losing You" video going, "What the f*ck is this?" Melina is visual. They're both like, insane, and I feel very blessed to catch these people at this point in their careers when they are figuring stuff out. I feel very blessed that they've allowed me to be a part of it."

Switching Between Accents

"It's not hard… more of your brain is being used. There will be words you'll come across and you're like, "What's that one?" You're learning as you go; "That doesn't feel right, that doesn't feel right." "Why doesn't this person understand me?" You just got to be in it the whole time. Back in the day I used to just stay in action for the whole experience, but I don't do that anymore."

Jateme's American Accent from *Widows* vs. Slim's American Accent

"It's the energy behind the accent. The entitlement behind the accent. It's a different energy to Slim, who is more accommodating and less assertive. But he can still stand up for himself.

I'm proper weird, I'll type in the home town on Instagram, and then I'll find people talking to camera on Instagram. So then I'll find a guy or couple guys and just rip the audio and listen to the audio of real people from the place. Because a lot of famous people are too affected, because they travel. You want it to feel rooted in some sort of thinking. That for me, it's about class, but it's about mentality as well. It's so related to how to speak and give that energy. Cleveland's a hard accent to do because you got the Rs."

What *Queen & Slim* Says About Gender Roles

"I think Slim is a guy that is more overtly masculine, and that's kind of what I wanted him to be. I wanted him to be when the film starts a Black woman in the audience would see him and go, "Huh." Because of how wishy-washy he can be at times. He obviously goes on a journey, but we assign assertion to masculinity, but it's just being a person that knows what they're about. That's what Queen has from the jump, she knows her plan. I think he finds his groove and his version of it and the stuff that he needs to grow in order to be the man that he wants.

There's a lot of stuff that is traditional. If you are taught that being a man is standing up for your own and you, and if you are put in a position where if you do, there's problems, it's shame, bruh. You want to riot but you can't express that in that space. So then that litters out on people closest to you. Your woman is going to feel that. She's gonna feel like if you're not working through those problems and emotions they're gonna feel…because then it causes a toxic dynamic because of that…not feeling empowered. Your idea of what your gender is and how people look at you. The intricacies of a police stop and all that stuff is really shaming. It's fucking dark."

Being the Martin to Queen's Malcolm

"I understand [the comparison]. I know you've seen her hair. What I find fascinating—and I can't say too much—is how that incident happens, flips on its head. As characters I completely understand. If Martin is forced to be violent for some reason, how does he feel about himself? How does he feel about what violence is now. I think there's an element for me, racism makes you fucking mad! It makes you paranoid. But it's some other person's problem, not my problem."

The Benefits of Going Dark

"I've done some dark stuff, but a lot of times I do these films and it's cathartic for me. I let sh*t out. That's all acting has been for me since I was very young, a safe space to let sh*t out. Because if I let it out on the streets…I was gifted that opportunity to kind of exercise certain emotions in certain forms. So it's like, "Great, I got it out of my system."

Interpreting the Ending of *Crouching Tiger Hidden Dragon*
by Stephen Cobbe[90]

Grappling with Jen's Decision

Nothing about *Crouching Tiger Hidden Dragon* astonishes me more than its ending. Our hero, standing atop Wudan Mountain, poised to realize everything she's struggled for, chooses instead to leap off its high peak, away from the lover and martial arts school that figure so prominently in her story.

As an eight year old, watching Zhang Ziyi's character jump off a cliff and into the clouds seemed a little silly to me, but no more so than the rest of the film, with its floating fight scenes that felt more out of *The Matrix* than Qing dynasty China.

But when I rewatched the film in high school, the ending felt out of place to me, almost jarring. Here was a mainstream, critical and commercial success whose conclusion, if taken literally, was the protagonist's suicide. I'd heard many people sing the film's praises, highlighting its beautiful love story, breathtaking cinematography, and ensemble performances. But never had I heard it described as tragic.

Even more puzzling to me was the simple question of why. Why had Jen, upon ridding herself of her familial obligations and

---

[90] Since high school, I've been passionate about interpreting stories. Whether it's in films, books, or video games, I think trying to understand what motivates characters stimulates reflection and emotional growth. I love how a story can transport you for a few hours to someone else's lived experience, which is often so different from your own. Roger Ebert put it succinctly when he called movies "empathy machines." They offer us the ability to connect with others across great distances. Through interpretation, we make stories a part of ourselves, as we attempt to connect them to our own life and understanding of the world. Although it's just a hobby for me right now, it's one that gives my life incredible meaning.

overbearing master(s), chosen not to return to the desert with her lover, nor continue her training at Wudan, nor even wander the landscape as a lone warrior like she did after fleeing her wedding, but instead hurl herself off a cliff?

Adding a cruel dimension to her decision were her final words to her lover, Lo, standing beside her:

Jen: "Do you remember the legend of the young man?"
Lo: "A faithful heart makes wishes come true."
Jen: "Make a wish, Lo."
Lo: (closing his eyes) "To be back in the desert, together again."

Jen dedicates her plunge to a wish she is perfectly able to fulfill herself. Her invocation of the young man, who in the legend sacrifices himself because of circumstances beyond his control to save his ailing parents, seems almost spiteful.

And yet, the camera paints a different picture. Jen's dramatic leap is more of a gentle glide, and her face remains calm and impassive as the clouds slowly subsume her body. As the film ends and the landscape of granite peaks slowly fades to black, it's hard not to feel like Jen has finally found peace.

Each time I've rewatched *Crouching Tiger Hidden Dragon*, I've tried to view the events of the film in the context of our hero's enigmatic final decision. The more I've watched, the more I've seen just how much change Jen undergoes as she seeks to reconcile the conflicting identities within her: governor's daughter, lover, apprentice, warrior, sister, and monk.

Understanding Jen's changing identity illuminates not only her character, but all the others, too. For while Jen, Li Mu Bai, Shu Lien, Lo, and Jade Fox each hail from different backgrounds, all of them bear the crushing social expectations of eighteenth century China.

Shortly before the film's end, a devastated Shu Lien, having failed to act on her feelings for Li Mu Bai before his death, exhorts Jen to be true to herself. The rest of this blog post is dedicated to understanding why, for Jen, being true to herself meant jumping off Wudan Mountain.

The Governor's Daughter

Of all the roles Jen plays, she is most socially accepted—and encumbered — as governor's daughter. Here, she is rarely shown outside the confines of her plush indoor quarters or horse-drawn carriage. She is outfitted in luxurious clothing and makeup, restricted to suitable activities like calligraphy, and carefully watched over by her parents, attendants, and Jade Fox. When it comes to marriage, her father chooses her husband for her, to maximize the benefit to his own career.

In Jen's first encounter with Shu Lien, her feeling of suffocation is evident:

Jen: "You're not married, are you?"
Shu "Lien: What do you think?"
Jen: "No! You couldn't roam around freely if you were."
Shu Lien: "You're probably right."

And later:

Jen: "I wish I were like the heroes in the books I read. Like you and Li Mu Bai. I guess I'm happy to be marrying. But to be free to live my own life, to choose whom I love: that is true happiness."

To escape the stifling confines of her life, Jen secretly trains to be a fighter with her master, Jade Fox. When the reality of her arranged marriage becomes too much to bear, she flees her family to roam the countryside as a warrior.

The Lover

In the deserts of western China, far away from the rigid society in Beijing, Jen discovers her first taste of true freedom. She finds in the bandit Lo someone with as fiery and untamed a spirit as her own. At first, their love is passionate, punctuated by violence and attempts to physically dominate one another. But soon it blossoms into a warm and intimate connection. For a time, the two live happily together in their desert fantasy.

Eventually, though, the reality of their class differences sets in. The governor's soldiers, out looking for Jen, begin to close in on Lo and his bandits.

"Don't send me back!" Jen begs Lo. Lo realizes that even if they could stay together in the desert, Jen would eventually grow "tired of this life." He vows to renounce his criminal ways and establish himself legitimately, with the hope of one day earning the respect of Jen's parents.

But society sees Lo only as a criminal, and everywhere he goes, his ability to start anew is thwarted. When he eventually returns empty-handed to Beijing, Lo discovers that Jen's feelings for him have changed. Exactly what brought about this change is unclear. Perhaps Jen's relationship with Lo was always going to be a temporary fling for her. Perhaps she realized the class differences between them were prohibitive. Perhaps she recognized that her training and potential as a warrior could never be fully realized with him. It's also possible that for Jen, being beholden to *anyone* would unacceptably compromise her independence. Lo did have something of a possessive streak. When they part ways in the desert, he announces to her, "I want you to be mine forever." Later, after Jen spurns Lo in Beijing, a disbelieving Shu Lien asks Lo if he really thought Jen would just "give it all up and go back West" with him. "She's mine," is all he manages to say in response.

Another complication in Jen's relationship with Lo is Li Mu Bai. Despite Li Mu Bai's clear feelings for Shu Lien, the budding master-apprentice relationship between him and Jen is fraught with emotion, and at times is even romantic.

"I knew she would intrigue you," Shu Lien says to Li Mu Bai, with a tinge of jealousy, as they discuss Jen.

As with Jen and Lo, social expectations stifle the love between Shu Lien and Li Mu Bai. For both, the dead cast a long shadow. Shu Lien feels obligated to suppress her feelings for Li Mu Bai in memory of her deceased fiancé, Li Mu Bai's brother. Li Mu Bai feels obligated to pursue vengeance for his deceased master, killed by Jade Fox, even if it costs him his life, as well as his opportunity to be with Shu Lien.

The Apprentice

In many ways, Li Mu Bai is the teacher Jen has needed her entire life. His mastery of the Wudan curriculum and his strong code of ethics contrast him sharply with her master, Jade Fox.

But Li Mu Bai seems oblivious to the misogynistic legacy of Wudan, which weighs heavily on Jade Fox and Jen. Because of the school's male-only admissions policy, talented women like Shu Lien and Jade Fox have had to hone their ability outside of Wudan, leaving them vulnerable to exploitation:

Li Mu Bai: "You stole a secret manual and poisoned our master! Now it's time for you to pay!"

Jade Fox: "Your master underestimated us women. Sure, he'd sleep with me, but he would never teach me. He deserved to die by a woman's hand!"

Jade Fox's experience challenges not only the villainous portrayal of her, but also the honor of Li Mu Bai's quest for vengeance.

Because of the toxic relationship of the prior generation — between Jen's master and Li Mu Bai's master — it's all but impossible for Jen to submit herself to Li Mu Bai's teachings. During their fights, every attempt by Li Mu Bai to impart a lesson on Jen is rebuffed. At one point, Jen cries out, "Wudan is a whorehouse! Keep your lessons!"

So poisoned is Jen's perception of Wudan that when she visits Shu Lien at her company headquarters, the mere suggestion that she rendezvous with Lo at Wudan causes her to challenge Shu Lien to armed combat.

Jen's fear of exploitation by Li Mu Bai is not unfounded. Without even a formal master-apprentice relationship, a romantic connection between Li Mu Bai and Jen begins to grow. All of their fight scenes are physical and intimate, but none more so than their clash in the bamboo forest, where the supple trees bend together under the weight of each warrior, bringing them face to face, within inches of one another.

So palpable is their romantic tension that when Li Mu Bai later discovers Jen in a drug-induced state, she bares her breasts to him, asking, "Is it me or the sword you want?"

The Warrior

Jen reaches the height of her freedom after she absconds from her wedding. Even in the desert, Jen was bound to Lo. Now, free of her family, lover, and masters, she roams the countryside as a warrior, living out the fantasy she described to Shu Lien in an earlier conversation:

Jen: "It must be exciting to be a fighter, to be totally free!"
Shu Lien: "Fighters have rules too: friendship, trust, integrity. Without rules, we wouldn't survive for long."
Jen: "I've read all about people like you. Roaming wild, beating up anyone who gets in your way!"

As she comes across an inn frequented by fighters, Jen seems determined to single-handedly tear down the patriarchal warrior society around her. Openly mocking the title-obsessed male fighters with overblown names like Iron Arm Mi and Shining Phoenix Mountain Gou, she slashes and bludgeons until no one is left to oppose her, at which point she vows to "kick over Wudan Mountain."

Even in this cathartic violence, though, she is still reminded of the larger society and her place in it, despite her best attempts to avoid it. When one of the fighters, recognizing Li Mu Bai's sword in her hand, asks if she is related to the great fighter, she lies and says that he is her defeated foe. When another asks if she is related to his master, Southern Crane — the same man who exploited her own master, Jade Fox — she feigns ignorance before mocking him. Finally, when someone introduces himself with the same last name as her fiancé, she is so incensed to even be reminded of her arranged marriage that she launches into a violent frenzy.

The Sister

Perhaps the most complex relationship in the story is that of Jen and Shu Lien. Although Jen violently clashes with all those close to her, what makes her fight with Shu Lien remarkable is how similar the two are, and how seemingly little cause they have for conflict. Both Jen and Shu Lien are talented female fighters living in a society that minimizes their ability. Both, too, are hostages to social pressures that dictate whom they should love.

Of all those in Jen's life, Shu Lien seems to be the only one with no designs on possessing her in one form or another. Such is the intimacy between the two that toward the end of the film, Jen starts referring to Shu Lien as "sister."

For all the commonality they share, though, there is an underlying tension between them that eventually explodes into violence. For Jen, Shu Lien and Jade Fox embody two feminine extremes: total compliance and total resistance. Their respective worldviews pull Jen in opposite directions, leaving her somewhere between the two, often unstable and with no clear direction.

Shu Lien represents the pinnacle of what a woman can achieve working within the society. She is renowned as a fighter, successful as a business owner, and respected for dutifully honoring her dead fiancé with celibacy. Unlike Li Mu Bai who radiates power almost to the point of arrogance, Shu Lien constantly practices restraint, leaving her immense ability less obvious.

Jade Fox, on the other hand, represents everything a woman can achieve working outside the society. She is a feared fighter and does not answer to the same burdensome social expectations as Shu Lien. Operating on the fringes, Jade Fox resorts to underhanded fighting techniques such as the use of poison and traps. And yet, for all their differences in approach, neither woman achieves what they really want. Both are denied admission to Wudan. Jade Fox is relegated to the shadows of society, while Shu Lien is forced to hide in public.

Initially, Shu Lien seems to embrace this compromise. At almost every turn, she discourages Jen from stepping outside her social bounds. In their first conversation, Shu Lien dismisses Jen's questions about life as a fighter with patronizing responses like "You're just not used to handling [the sword]" or "You're too young to understand." Later, when Li Mu Bai suggests that Jen train at Wudan, Shu Lien is quick to reply that Wudan does not accept women. Even when Li Mu Bai indicates an exception could be made for Jen, Shu Lien falls back on another patriarchal excuse, saying that Jen's husband might object to her studying there. Finally, when Jen arrives on her doorstep after her violent rampage, Shu Lien advises Jen simply to return to her family rather than continuing to blaze her own path.

But after Li Mu Bai's death, her view changes. For all she achieved working within the society, Shu Lien becomes ambivalent about whether it was worth the steep cost. In her final words to Jen, Shu Lien no longer suggests a particular path to follow, but instead urges Jen simply to be true to herself.

The Monk

Throughout the film, there is a tension between embracing the physical world, with all its accompanying desires, and withdrawing from it. For most of the film, though, it is Li Mu Bai, not Jen, who wrestles with this spiritual question. During his first visit to Shu Lien, Li Mu Bai confesses that his meditation did not bring him the peace he expected:

Li Mu Bai: "I came to a place of deep silence. I was surrounded by light. Time and space disappeared. I had come to a place my master had never told me about."
Shu Lien: "You were enlightened?"
Li Mu Bai: "No. I didn't feel the bliss of enlightenment. Instead, I was surrounded by an endless sorrow. I couldn't bear it. I broke off my meditation. I couldn't go on. There was something pulling me back."

Although he leaves his meditation to pursue his love for Shu Lien, Li Mu Bai can't seem to fully commit to the physical world, the world of sensation. In a later conversation with Shu Lien, as she passes him a cup of tea, their fingers touch. Embarrassed, Li Mu Bai pulls back:

Li Mu Bai: "Shu Lien, the things we touch have no permanence. My master would say there is nothing we can hold on to in this world. Only by letting go can we truly possess what is real."

> *Shu Lien:* "*Not everything is an illusion. My hand, wasn't that real?*"
> *Li Mu Bai:* "*Your hand, rough and calloused from machete practice. All this time, I've never had the courage to touch it.*"

He even denies the physical reality of his powerful sword, the Green Destiny:

> *Li Mu Bai:* "*Like most things, I am nothing. It's the same for this sword. All of it is simply a state of mind.*"
> *Jen:* "*Stop talking like a monk! Just fight!*"

At one point, to demonstrate to Jen the sword's supposed worthlessness, he flings it off a waterfall.

Yet, when the Green Destiny is returned to Li Mu Bai after Jen steals it, he admits, "Getting it back makes me realize how much I'd missed it."

It's clear that power resides in the physical sword itself. During Jen's rampage at the inn, each of the fighters watch helplessly as the Green Destiny splits their weapons into pieces. When Jen and Shu Lien come to blows, Shu Lien, the more experienced fighter, is forced to repeatedly retrieve new weapons to replace those destroyed by Jen's sword.

"Without the Green Destiny, you are nothing," she exasperatedly tells Jen. Complementing the sword is Jen's comb, the other prominent physical object in the story. Whereas the Green Destiny is the physical embodiment of Jen's warrior identity, the comb is the embodiment of her identity as a lover. As the sword repeatedly changes hands between her and Li Mu Bai, so too does the comb, between her and Lo, reflecting the ebb and flow of each identity within her.

As the film reaches its climax, both Li Mu Bai and Jen finally resolve their relationship to the physical world, but in dramatically different ways. For Li Mu Bai, this occurs in his dying moments:

Li Mu Bai: "My life is departing. I've only one breath left."

Shu Lien: "Use it to meditate. Free yourself from this world as you have been taught. Let your soul rise to eternity with your last breath. Do not waste it for me."

Li Mu Bai: "I've already wasted my whole life. I want to tell you with my last breath: I have always loved you."

After his death, a heartbroken Shu Lien, having let the love of her life slip through her fingers, approaches Jen:

Shu Lien: "Now you must go to Wudan Mountain. Lo awaits you there. Promise me one thing, whatever path you take in this life, be true to yourself."

With Shu Lien's entreaty hanging over her, Jen reunites with Lo one last time and tearfully makes love to him, before leaving behind her comb. Having relinquished both sword and comb, Jen leaps from Wudan Mountain, away from the physical world forever.

Crouching Tiger, Hidden Dragon

The name of the film is taken from a Chinese idiom which describes a place or situation full of unnoticed masters. In one of the film's most poignant scenes, Shu Lien observes Jen, the governor's daughter, practicing calligraphy. From the deftness of her brushstrokes, Shu Lien concludes that Jen is more than she appears, that in fact she is the masked warrior from the night before. It is a moment rife with meaning and sadness.

Crouching Tiger Hidden Dragon is a story of stifled possibility, of lives lived with unrealized potential, where masters are forced to hide in plain sight to avoid the scrutiny of a society that rejects their desires.

Why did Jen jump off Wudan Mountain? Li Mu Bai's dying epiphany was a call to embrace, not reject, the physical world. To learn from the mistakes of the prior generation, Jen should pursue her love for Lo, if not continue her training at Wudan, or so it would seem.

But Jen's choices are poisoned by the larger society. To return to her family would be to forfeit her say in who she loved. To return to the desert would be to resign herself to a life on the run, possessed by Lo. To return to her training at Wudan would be to subject herself to the school's legacy of exploitation. And to return to the countryside as a roaming warrior would be to escape only temporarily, with her family and her past never far behind.

With all physical paths exhausted, Jen turns to a spiritual path. By choosing to withdraw from the world, she reestablishes her agency and her ability to make choices consistent with her values. In this way, Jen remains true to herself.

In a world where heroes can fly, it's unclear if the literal meaning of Jen's withdrawal is transcendence or self-annihilation.

But I like to think Jen's faithful heart means Lo's wish can still come true — perhaps not in this world, but some other, where, free from her father's soldiers and free to realize her unlimited potential as a warrior and a lover, she can return to the desert with Lo and be happy.

Waves: An Anti-Black Coming of Age Film

by Fatima Ali Omar[91]

Waves comes as the third feature from Director Trey Edward Shults and follows the story of a suburban African-American family in South Florida as they go through the trials and tribulations of life. This might sound fairly innocuous and yet, the film rapidly unravels under Shults' inability to capture his Black protagonist, Tyler Williams, realistically. Shults, who is white, fails to give his characters and by extension the film the nuance, depth or racial self-awareness that it so desperately needs.

The first half of the film is led by Kelvin Harrison Jr who plays Tyler Williams, a popular athlete training for the upcoming season under the harsh supervision of his father, played by Sterling K. Brown. The catalyst of the film is introduced when an injury puts a stop to Tyler's chances of winning a wrestling scholarship. It's from this moment on that Tyler's life begins to spiral: an unexpected pregnancy with his Latinx girlfriend Alexis, played by Alexa Demie, and the crumbling relationship with his father take center stage.

With a visual palette that evokes the likes of Moonlight (2016), also set in Florida, Shults' film employs swirling camerawork and gorgeous cinematography to mask its own shallowness under the guise of its more accomplished counterpart. Yet unlike the former, Waves has no idea how to evoke empathy for the constantly angry Tyler. Shults is unable to contextualize Tyler's anger or provide an interior framework to help us empathize with it. Moonlight is a

---

[91] Fatima Ali Omar a Screenwriter, filmmaker and freelancer writing and focusing on issues of race and gender in pop culture and cinema.

deep exploration of the multifaceted, complex and tender journey that is Black masculinity and the interior lives and relationships that fill up its three protagonists lives. Waves, however, is the antithesis of this. Tyler is relegated to a mere stereotype propped up by a painfully on the nose hip-hop centered soundtrack that comes across as a desperate attempt at adding validity to Tyler's race. Moments where his rage can be explained or contextualized became needle drops for the likes of Frank Ocean, Kendrick Lamar and Tyler The Creator. A particularly baffling example of this is when Alexis, Tyler's girlfriend, tells him over text that she is planning on going through with her pregnancy. Instead of unpacking this or offering us a glimpse into how this fits into the larger family dynamic, we are instead treated to Tyler trashing his room to the overpowering and intoxicating beat of Tyler The Creator's IFHY.

Shults is clearly unable to explore any nuanced unpacking of Tyler's rage that doesn't present itself externally or provide an opportunity to squeeze another popular hit rap song. It seems his concern is to provide a surface level presentation of Black masculinity that leans into stereotypes and is signified by a playlist crumbling under the weight of its own desperate attempt to appeal to its Black audience. Tyler is a one note character filled with anger. Anger at his father, anger at his injury, anger at his girlfriend. Shults fails to find any constructive or empathetic way to channel Tyler's anger, instead we see him rail against his girlfriend employing misogynistic language and eventually killing her during the climax of the first act in an alcohol fueled rage.

The issue with Waves is that it comes at a time when directors such as Barry Jenkins, Dee Rees, Jordan Peele (to name a few) are portraying Black life in all the complexity, tenderness and vivid interiority we deserve, on screen. Waves' portrayal and handling of its Black characters therefore is nothing short of lacking. The Williams family is caught in the whirlwind of Tyler's rage and it is this that dominates and shapes their lives. We are not privy to any of the internal aspirations this family has, nor are we privy to any facet of Tyler's personality that isn't colored by misogyny and violence. To center a story around an African-American family is to take responsibility for telling this story with the nuance and racial awareness that it demands. In an interview with Deadline, Shults described the film as 'deeply personal' a statement which is not damning in and of itself. However, it becomes so when it is superimposed onto the life of a Black family with no nuance or understanding of the way Black men in particular have historically been portrayed on screen.

Waves is not the first film to be made by a white director who only examines Black life through a simplified framework, unloading trauma onto Black and brown bodies to emotionally manipulate its audience. However, it is a particularly startling addition to the current cinematic landscape that we have started to adjust ourselves to. Now more than ever the question of who should tell Black stories is imperative to ask. More importantly why films like Waves helmed by white directors continue to be greenlit in lieu of Black filmmakers with more nuanced and empathetic ways of portraying Black life on screen.

Tyler's misogyny is not egregious in the sense that it exists but rather due to it becoming his defining characteristic: we aren't privy to his internal emotions much less his aspirations outside of sports and the pressure of his father. A conversation early on in the film becomes the only marker that Shults is aware of his protagonists race when Tyler's father states they have to be 'better than average'. Waves is simply incapable of handling the race of its protagonist because it doesn't understand how it informs his life, instead resorting to oft repeated statements like the former to masquerade as being informed on the topic. Even then, the film holds contempt for its Black and Latinx cast, when they are not presented as violent they are being killed or punished for the simple fact of their existence.

A film of two halves, Waves leaves Tyler's story abruptly as he is holed up in prison and, apart from a single shot towards the end of the film, we never return to his character. This is both a merciful and disappointing choice as Tyler's story ends with incarceration and it falls on his grieving family to unpack this trauma. The latter half of Waves focuses on its white character Luke, played by Lucas Hedges.

Luke begins a summer romance with Tyler's sister Emily, played by Taylor Russell. The two embark on a road trip to help Luke overcome the anger he feels towards his abusive alcoholic dad and forgive him before he dies of cancer. Where Tyler was presented as an explosive, misogynistic and violent teen, Luke is given the time to build and overcome the anger he feels towards his father.

Despite appearing in the middle of the film, Luke is provided with more interiority, empathy and nuance than either Tyler or his family. Scene after scene of Black trauma follows Tyler's incarceration as his mother, played brilliantly by Renée Elise Goldsberry, begins to lose control of her business and marriage. Even then, Shults offers no respite to his Black characters, where Luke gets his sun soaked montages, the Williams marriage is unravelling and the only consistent character beat becomes tragedy.

Waves does not understand the interiority of its Black characters lives, instead of attempting empathy it slides into trauma porn. Even more glaring is that Tyler is not offered the agency to personally deal with his internal demons, instead he becomes a forgotten character we never hear directly from again.

The saving grace of this film is Taylor Russell's quietly nuanced and emotional performance as Emily. Waves is at its best when it doesn't attempt to understand or shallowly explore black masculinity and family dynamics. When the film focuses on forgiveness for Tyler from his family, it shines through as a tentative exploration on how to reconcile our relationship to our loved ones who've committed the most heinous of crimes. Even then, these moments are too fleeting to rise up from the constant barrage of pain the Williams family undergoes. It is a wonder then why the film devotes its first half to Tyler's character when it is so opposed to directly giving him the nuance and empathy a topic like this requires.

To call this film anti-black would not be an overstatement as it clumsily handles the representation of its Black teen, resorting to painting him in the hyper-violent and misogynistic stereotypes we are all too familiar with. Shults absolves himself and the audience of confronting Tyler's humanity by locking him in a prison cell and ripping his agency away from him. Instead Waves pivots to what feels like a completely different film in the second half, that juxtaposes Black and white masculinity in naive and ultimately racist ways.

Waves is not a surprising film in that it is exactly the end result you would get when a white filmmaker makes a film about a Black family despite having no understanding, context or range to confront the reality of being Black. It is simply disappointing to see it so roundly praised when its portrayal is propped up by racist stereotypes that give no thought to the possibility that there is more to Tyler than this rootless rage.

Miyazaki's Beautiful Antiwar Dreams

by Dan Sanchez[92]

War and peace in the films of Studio Ghibli.

It is the last year of the Second World War. American bombers drop napalm canisters on Kobe, Japan, setting the picturesque city of wood, canvas, and paper alight. A young mother is caught in the conflagration, suffers greatly, then succumbs to her disfiguring burns. With the father fighting at sea, her adolescent son Seita must fend for himself and for his 5-year old sister Setsuko as famine stalks the country. In spite of all his efforts, Seita must watch as Setsuko, an imaginative, fun-loving child, becomes emaciated, sickens, weakens, and eventually dies of malnutrition.

This is the story told in Studio Ghibli's 1988 animated film *Grave of the Fireflies*, and it is no less harrowing and haunting for being a "cartoon." As Roger Ebert wrote in his 4-star review[93]:

> "'Grave of the Fireflies' is an emotional experience so powerful that it forces a rethinking of animation. (…) 'Grave of the Fireflies' is a powerful dramatic film that happens to be animated, and I know what the critic Ernest Rister means when he compares it to 'Schindler's List' and says, 'It is the most profoundly human animated film I've ever seen.' (…)
> Yes, it's a cartoon, and the kids have eyes like saucers, but it belongs on any list of the greatest war films ever made."

---

[92] Dan Sanchez is the Director of Content at the Foundation for Economic Education (FEE) and the editor-in chief of FEE.org.
[93] Ebert, Roger, "Review: Grave of The Fireflies," Roger Ebert (March 19, 2000) https://www.rogerebert.com/reviews/great-movie-grave-of-the-fireflies-1988.

The director Isao Takahata has denied its characterization as an anti-war film. But as Clint Eastwood has said, "any war told realistically is an anti-war movie." And *Fireflies* is unsparing in its portrayal of the realities of war, especially for being based on a semi-autobiographical novel, whose author lost his adoptive father to the firebombing of Kobe and afterward had to watch his baby sister Keiko die of hunger.

Kobe was only one of the 67 Japanese cities burned by the United States Air Force, under the direction of Curtis LeMay. Nicknamed "the Demon," LeMay was instrumental in the US shift from high-altitude bombing with general purpose explosives to the low-altitude incendiary bombing of Japanese cities that resulted in hundreds of thousands of civilian deaths and the famine-inducing ruination of the economy. He later became a tireless advocate for bombing Vietnam, as he put it, "back to the Stone Age," and for bombing the whole world back to the Ice Age by launching a nuclear first strike against the Soviet Union.

LeMay also oversaw and championed the enforcement of the total blockade of Japan by filling the waters around its port cities with aerial-dropped mines, which, for example, caused shipping through Kobe to plummet by 85%. This campaign was dubbed, with a refreshing lack of hypocrisy, "Operation Starvation." Thus, the starvation of little Setsuko/Keiko was not "collateral damage," but a premeditated murder.

When Leslie Stahl asked Madeline Albright about the half-million Iraqi children deprived to death by US sanctions ("more children than died in Hiroshima"), the then Secretary of State famously answered "we think the price is worth it." Of course elite war-bringers like LeMay and Albright do not themselves pay the "prices" they decide are acceptable. The costs of their decisions are externalized onto the victims of their economic and shooting wars.

Fireflies tells the story of two children who actually paid the "price." That is why it is such a powerfully anti-war film regardless of the director's intentions. It tells the story of war realistically from the perspective of its most vulnerable victims, as opposed to just the "derring-do" of fighters. And that is more than enough to inspire any decent human being to curse the name of war upon watching it. More specifically, it will move any heart not corrupted and hardened by nationalism to look on policies like the Israeli blockade of Gaza, US sanctions on Iran, and the new Saudi blockade of Yemen, as the infanticidal atrocities they are.

Takahata co-founded Studio Ghibli with Hayao Miyazaki, and the anti-war message in Miyazaki's work is more subtle, yet also much more deliberate.

In western fantasy, wars are traditionally depicted as worthy struggles between unalloyed good and pure evil, with the protagonist firmly on the side of the angels and against the devils. Even *The Lord of the Rings* trilogy falls victim to this tendency, as George R.R. Martin has pointed out.[94] In Miyazaki's fantasies, however, wars are portrayed as senseless and horrible. The heroes are generally not on either side of the war, but are caught between the two. And their struggle is not to win the war, but to defuse it.

The characters who pursue war — generally government officials — are portrayed as vainglorious and arrogant schemers who rashly court cataclysm for the sake of their grandiose ambitions.

Yet even these antagonists are not treated as devils, but as deeply flawed human beings. The heroes do not harbor vendettas and thirst for vengeance against them, as the typical western action hero does. Rather, the heroes try to convince them to abandon their disastrous plans, while also striving to foil those plans directly. The climax of the film comes not with the hero impaling or detonating his foe, as in so many Hollywood movies, or in the villain falling to

---

[94] Gunner, Shaun, "George R.R. Martin asks: "What was Aragorn's tax policy?", *The Tolkien Society* (April 24, 2014)
https://www.tolkiensociety.org/2014/04/grrm-asks-what-was-aragorns-tax-policy/.

his doom, as in so many Disney animated films. Miyazaki's heroes achieve victory, not through the destruction of their enemies, but by foiling their plans enough such that the belligerents finally relent. The loving and forgiving attitude of the hero sometimes even prevails to the point of converting villains into friends.

"Stop! Don't kill any more!"

Miyazaki's first and most paradigmatic masterpiece was initially written by him as a comic (manga) and then scripted and directed by him as an animated film (anime) shortly before Studio Ghibli was founded. In *Nausicaä of the Valley of the Wind* (1984), two post-apocalyptic kingdoms, Tolumekia and Pejite, are locked in an existential struggle over control of an ancient weapon of mass destruction called a "Giant Warrior." The struggle becomes so desperate that one side is even willing to almost completely destroy itself for the sake of completely destroying the other side. Here we see a portrayal of the Dr. Strangelovean logic of men like LeMay, written by a man from the only country that has thus far been attacked with nuclear weapons. One of the characters even defends the mad ploy by saying, "It's to protect the world. Please understand."

Another factor in the war is the Ohmu: a race of giant, nigh-invulnerable semi-sentient bugs. The Ohmu are herd creatures that lethally stampede when enraged by violence perpetrated against their own kind. As Randolph Bourne taught, this is basically what happens to human beings as well when they develop war fever, especially when provoked by atrocity stories (whether real or manufactured). For more on this, see my essay "The Herd Mind."[95] At one point, this characteristic of the Ohmu is deliberately stimulated and exploited by the government of one of the war-

---

[95] Sanchez, Dan, "The Herd Mind," *Medium* (April 3, 2015) https://medium.com/dan-sanchez/the-herd-mind-64127f5bac9f.

ring kingdoms, just as real-life governments and other terrorist organizations exploit and engineer atrocities so as to induce war fever. For more on this, see my essay "The Symbiosis of Savagery."[96]

Nausicaä is an earnest, peace-loving young princess who becomes embroiled in the war between the two kingdoms when the Giant Warrior crash lands in her little country, which is then brought under the brutal military occupation of the imperial Tolumekians for the purpose of securing the WMD. Even after her homeland is attacked by both kingdoms, she strives for peace and understanding, going so far as to save the lives of members of both royal houses. And rather than try to destroy the rampaging Ohmu, she endeavors to stop the crime against their young that is provoking their violent rage (blowback) in the first place.

The first official Studio Ghibli production was Miyazaki's *Castle in the Sky* (1986). As in Nausicaä, the chief villains are agents and soldiers of an imperial government, hellbent on rediscovering and exploiting an ancient weapon of mass destruction. And like Princess Nausicaä, the young heroes of *Castle in the Sky*, Princess Sheeta and Pazu, seek to avert war, in this case by destroying the WMD.

> *"What exactly are you here for?"*
> *"To see with eyes unclouded by hate."*

In *Princess Mononoke*, the chief hero is Prince Ashitaka, who, like Nausicaä, is thrust into world affairs when his little country is impacted by the spillover effects of a war abroad. And like Nausicaä, he strives to defuse the conflict instead of taking a side in it. At one point, one character asks in bafflement, "Whose side is he on?" The most representative image of this characteristic of the Miyazaki hero is the moment when Ashitaka steps between

---

[96] Sanchez, Dan, "The Symbiosis of Savagery," *Medium* (March 1, 2015) https://medium.com/dan-sanchez/the-symbiosis-of-savagery-68d5b75b6e70

the main figures of both sides of the war, and prevents them from killing each other, even at the cost of grievous injury to himself.

Throughout the film, warlike hatred is portrayed as a mystical, contagious, fatal disease that materializes as a black ooze and turns rational beings into rampaging, brute beasts. Again, think of Bourne's "Herd Mind" concept.

> *"Is it the enemy's or one of ours?"*
> *"What difference does it make? Stupid murderers."*

Miyazaki was so angered by the Iraq War that for a time he boycotted travel to America. He said that his outrage over the war had a major influence on his *Howl's Moving Castle* (2004). That film centers around a war between two neighboring countries (repeatedly referred to as "this stupid war") in which even magicians have been enlisted. Howl is a draft-dodging renegade magician who stays free by roving from place to place in an ambulating, teleporting magico-mechanical castle and by keeping multiple identities. When asked by his beloved Sophie how many aliases he has, he answers, "as many as I need to keep my freedom."

One side of the war is masterminded by a Palpatine/Dick Cheney-like sorceress who had originally trained Howl. Now, she wants her errant "Sith" disciple either conscripted, drained of his powers, or dead. She serves as sort of a magical prime minister to the country's king, a ridiculous figure who boyishly exults over his war and fancies himself a brilliant strategist. I strongly suspect Miyazaki had George W. Bush in mind when creating this character.

When Howl finally does intervene in the war, he does so, not by partaking in the slaughter of civilians perpetrated by both sides, but by wrecking the weapons of war being used for that slaughter.

The film's most glorious moment is when Howl and Sophie see a flying battleship appear and violate the beautiful serenity of his long-time refuge: a lovely little cottage amid a field of flowers.

Howl: "What is that thing doing out here?"
Sophie: "A battleship?"
Howl: "Looking for more cities to burn."
Sophie: "Is it the enemy's or one of ours?"
Howl: "What difference does it make? Those stupid murderers."

Then, with a wave of his hand, Howl disables the ship by magically disconnecting its wiring. This is Miyazaki at his finest. The bombing of cities is mass murder, regardless of whether it is done by our government in our name or by "the enemy."

In *Howl,* as in both *Nausicaä* and *Mononoke,* true victory comes, not from the conquest of one war belligerent by another, but by both simply choosing to cease to fight, having seen the futility of the war, thanks to the exploits of the heroes.

"I'd rather be a pig than a fascist."

A similarly anti-military, anti-nationalist, and anti-conscription note is struck in *Porco Rosso* (1992), a story about a former World War I Italian fighter pilot who is transformed into a humanoid pig, foreswears military flying and war profiteering, and embarks on a career in private security.

My favorite scene in this movie involves a surreptitious meeting Porco has with an old friend in a movie theater in Fascist Italy.

Porco Rosso: You're a major, eh? You've come up in the world, Fierrali.
Fierrali: You fool. Why did you come back?
Porco Rosso: I make it a rule to go wherever I want to.

Fierrali: The authorities aren't going to let you go this time. Did somebody tail you?
Porco Rosso: I gave them the slip.
Fierrali: A warrant for your arrest is being issued for refusal to cooperate
with the state, illegal coming and going, decadent thoughts, being a lazy pig, and display of indecent materials...
Porco Rosso: Ha ha ha ha
Fierrali: You idiot, this is no time to laugh. They're threatening to confiscate your fighter.
Porco Rosso: This is a terrible film.
Fierrali: Marco, come back to the Air Force. We'll use our influence to work
something out for you.
Porco Rosso: I'd rather be a pig than a fascist.
Fierrali: The age of daredevil aviators is over. Now we can only fly in the
service of worthless causes like "country" or "nation".
Porco Rosso: I only fly for myself.

Bretigne Shaffer has written an excellent appreciation of the film, in which she wrote:

"When he makes a large cash withdrawal from the bank, the teller asks him if he wants to make a contribution "to the people" with a Patriot Bond.

"I'm not a person," is Porco's terse reply.

Later, when his arms merchant warns him that the government may pass laws against what he does, he replies "laws don't apply to pigs." (After Porco leaves, the merchant's son asks "how's war different from bounty hunting?" His father replies "war profiteers are villains. Bounty hunters are just stupid.)"

Anti-fascist, renegade, capitalist, pig. Porco Rosso is one of Miyazaki's greatest characters: a veritable Malcolm Reynolds with a snout.

Miyazaki is now retired. His final film, *The Wind Rises* is a beautifully fitting swan song in two ways. For one, it is perhaps his most expressly anti-war film. For another, it is his most clearly expressed paean to the splendor and tragedy of human flight.

The film is a fictionalized telling of the life of Jiro Horikoshi, the inventor of the Japanese World War II dogfighter the Mitsubishi A5M and its successor the A6M "Zero." Miyazaki was inspired to make *The Wind Rises* when he read that Horikoshi had allegedly once muttered, "All I wanted to do was to make something beautiful."

"Mei, we're the wind!"

The exhilarating beauty and freedom of human flight is a theme that pervades Miyazaki's entire corpus, including his films that do not address war.

One such film, *My Neighbor Totoro* was released simultaneously with *Grave of the Fireflies*. It is Studio Ghibli's and Miyazaki's signature film. It tells of hope and joy in the face of childhood adversity just as movingly as its counterpart tells of despair and grief. Satsuki, a girl about Seita's age, and her sister Mei, a girl about Setsuko's age, both struggle with their mother's serious illness and long absence. Like Setsuko, Mei comes into peril in spite of her older sibling's efforts to protect her. But since this story is 20th century fantasy, and not a biographical tale set in the actual history of that grim century, things play out very differently. Rather than "aid" from a wicked and incompetent government (like the rice dole in *Fireflies*), the children receive saving help from forest spirits, including especially the giant, furry Totoro.

At one point, the Totoro takes the two girls flying through the air on its magic, spinning top. As they soar unseen over their neighbors, and rustle crops in the field as they pass, Satsuki exclaims in delight, "Mei, we're the wind!"

Similarly exhilarating moments can be found in Miyazaki's *Kiki's Delivery Service* (flying on a broom), *Whisper of the Heart* (riding the wind with a humanoid cat), and *Spirited Away* (a flying dragon). When Howl first meets Sophie they walk on air together. Nausicaä, Sheeta, and Pazu ride the wind on gliders. And of course Porco Rosso soars through the air in his plane.

"Airplanes are beautiful cursed dreams, waiting for the sky to swallow them up."

Miyazaki is clearly enchanted with flight and the wind. He generously shares that enchantment with us by translating it into beautiful films. In *The Wind Rises*, he portrays Jiro Horikoshi as similarly enchanted with the beauty of aircraft. He has Jiro meet, in shared dreams, his hero, the Italian aircraft designer Giovanni Battista Caproni. Caproni teaches him that "Airplanes are beautiful dreams," but warns him that they are also "cursed dreams."

Nobody is more familiar with what a curse airplanes can be when deployed for evil than the Japanese. Airplanes dropped the canisters that burned their cities, the mines that starved their children, and the nukes that instantly made vast irradiated graveyards out of Hiroshima and Nagasaki — for the first time in history visiting solar-temperature hell upon human habitations, and hinting at mankind's full capacity for suicidal madness.

But their intimate familiarity with the "cursed dream" of airplanes also stems from the Japanese state's own misuse of the great invention for its imperial dreams. This truth is intimated throughout *The Wind Rises* in the tension between the desire of several of the characters to simply build graceful, well-designed aircraft and the knowledge that their beautiful creations will be used to perpetrate the hideous horrors of war.

When Jiro first meets Caproni in their shared dream space, Jiro is just a boy and Caproni's Italy is embroiled in World War I. They look up at Italian biplanes departing into the sky. A gunner salutes them. Caproni says:

"Look at them. They will bomb an enemy city. Most of them will never return. Well, it will all be over soon."

The scene cuts to an image of one of the planes crashing into a burning city. But Caproni insists that "airplanes are not tools for war." The two board a different kind of plane and take off. Caproni explains:

"This is my true dream. When the war is over, I will build this. What do you think? Magnificent, isn't she? Instead of bombs, she'll carry passengers."

They climb out onto the wing, where Caproni shows Jiro an even grander plane, filled with happy tourists.

"She is beautiful, yes? She will carry 100 people across the Atlantic, both ways!"

Caproni's true dream is to give people the joy and freedom of air travel: to use his creations, not to slay, but to serve[97] his fellow human beings.

Jiro is dazzled and deeply affected. Years later, Mitsubishi sends Jiro and his friend Honjo to study Nazi Germany's G38 passenger plane, which the company plans to purchase and convert into a bomber. Echoing Caproni's sentiment, Jiro remarks:

---

[97] Sanchez, Dan, "Capitalism Encapsulated," Medium (January 17, 2015) https://medium.com/dan-sanchez/capitalism-encapsulated-c33d963d2a2e.

"Look, passengers sit in the wings. It'd be a shame to put bombs there."

In another dream-meeting in the middle of Jiro's career, Caproni says:

"Humanity has always dreamed of flying. But the dream is cursed. My aircraft are destined to become tools for slaughter and destruction."

The fictional Jiro then echoes his historical counterpart, saying:

"I just want to create beautiful airplanes,"

Later, during a planning meeting with his design team attended by his bosses, he discusses how weight is a big problem for one of the possible designs. He half-jokingly, half-hopefully proposes:

"One solution could be: we could leave out the guns."

Of course, everyone bursts into laughter, and Jiro moves on to the next design.

Before World War II even began, Japan was already using its new planes to try to crush a Chinese rebellion against its imperial yoke by terror bombing major Chinese cities, burning and asphyxiating thousands of civilians. Then, goaded by the American-led embargo of its islands, the planes were used to attack Pearl Harbor, as well as British and Dutch colonial holdings in Asia. Taking the American bait, and thinking that inflicting such a blow would induce Washington to negotiate an end to the embargo was a spectacularly disastrous miscalculation. The Japanese policy makers fatally underestimated both America's industrial capacity and its political class's appetite for blood and empire. Now Washington had just the excuse it needed to overwhelm domestic opposition and visit hell upon Japan for the sake of establishing its hegemony over east Asia. The real-life Horikoshi himself wrote in his diary:

"When we awoke on the morning of December 8, 1941, we found ourselves — without any foreknowledge — to be embroiled in war... Since then, the majority of us who had truly understood the awesome industrial strength of the United States never really believed that Japan would win this war. We were convinced that surely our government had in mind some diplomatic measures which would bring the conflict to a halt before the situation became catastrophic for Japan. But now, bereft of any strong government move to seek a diplomatic way out, we are being driven to doom. Japan is being destroyed. I cannot do [anything] other but to blame the military hierarchy and the blind politicians in power for dragging Japan into this hellish cauldron of defeat."

The Empire of Japan's imminent use of their advanced planes in foolish aggression and its disastrous consequences are continually foreshadowed throughout the film.

A friendly German expatriate named Castorp warns Jiro:

"Make the world your enemy? Forget it. Japan will blow up. Germany will blow up, too."

Later, Honjo shares with Jiro his frustrations over his work designing Japan's first advanced bomber. Jiro asks, "And who are they going to bomb with it?" Honjo answers wearily, "China, Russia, Britain, the Netherlands, America." Jiro echoes Castorp, darkly predicting, "Japan will blow up."

After much of Japan does blow up, Jiro and Caproni meet one last time. After walking through the wreckage of his planes amid a bombed-out city, he mourns that his "kingdom of dreams" has become a "land of the dead." They look up together as a squadron of Jiro's planes ascend into the sky. Caproni congratulates Jiro for finally completing his masterpiece of graceful flight. In a moment that bookends their first meeting, one of the pilots salutes Jiro. "Not a single one returned," Jiro says. "There was nothing to return to," Caproni responds, referring to the devastation of Japan. "Airplanes are beautiful cursed dreams, waiting for the sky to swallow them up."

The beautiful/cursed dream of flight dichotomy can be found throughout the Miyazaki/Studio Ghibli catalog. In *Nausicaä*, there are graceful gliders but also lumbering warships and Zero-like dogfighters. In *Castle in the Sky*, the characters fly in wondrous bug-wing aircraft, but are also strafed by warship cannons. And it turns out that the "Castle in the Sky" itself is a massive suborbital Death Star that deploys an entire armada of killer drones.

Just as *Fireflies* vividly showed what World War II air raids did to the lovely cities of Japan, *Howl's Moving Castle* visually referenced the fate of the beautiful old European cities, like Dresden and Hamburg, that were firebombed in that war. The movie begins with the pomp and circumstance of patriotic war preparation. This nationalist virus lives amid the prosperity, activity, and commerce of a beautiful and bustling European port town. Tragically the virus kills its lovely host, as later we see the bombers that Howl worked to sabotage turn this jewel of civilization into a lake of fire. The human toll is not displayed nearly as graphically as in *Fireflies*, but the message is clear. The horrors of firebombing are given a reverse image in another scene in Howl, in which falling stars (dying fire spirits) create a beautifully illuminated display.

"Why do fireflies die so soon?"

A similar contrast can be found in *Fireflies*. As Ebert wrote of the napalm canisters at the beginning of the film:

"These bombs, longer than a tin can but about as big around, fall to earth trailing cloth tails that flutter behind them; they are almost a beautiful sight. After they hit, there is a moment's silence, and then they detonate, spraying their surroundings with flames."

This film's reverse image of firebombs are the fireflies that so enchant Setsuko. In a beautiful moment amid their tribulations, the brother and sister gather fireflies to dazzlingly illuminate the cave they are living in. Setsuko's look of wonder is heart-piercing.

But the magic disappears the next morning when she finds that the fireflies are all dead. This *memento mori* causes her to think of her mother. She buries the fireflies in a grave as she thinks her mother was buried, and asks her brother, "Why do fireflies die so soon?" The question foreshadows her own unbearably untimely death and the flickering brevity of her life. Life indeed is already so brief, which makes it all the more a crime for war bringers to make it even shorter for so many, and so painful in the duration.

Studio Ghibli is often called the Japanese Disney. Yet nothing in American animation can compare with it: not Disney, not even Pixar. The Miyazaki heroine, for example, is much more worthy of emulation than the Disney Princess. More than that, even most western fantasy cinema and literature in general pales in comparison, including much that we consider great. For example, as much as Tolkien's *Lord of the Rings* is a profound meditation on the corruption of power, its discussion of war and peace is crudely Manichean. Yet on this subject, and so many others, the fantasy of Studio Ghibli — *especially* the work of the creative genius Hayao Miyazaki— is wise and deeply moral, as well as exhilarating and achingly beautiful. It is a cultural treasure that stands and soars in a class of its own.

Miyazaki's films are beautiful dreams. May time never swallow them up.

Going to The Beginning - The Art of Screenwriting: 1910s
by Seraphima Bogomolova[98]

In writing there is a certain rule: if anything bothers you with the end of your story, go to the beginning of it and see if you have missed something, or if you have diverted from the chosen path on the way to the end. I find it extremely useful. It always works. I have applied the same formula to answer some questions about current screenwriting situation and where it is heading or, maybe not, by going to the very beginning of its story – the 1910s.

As cinema was an art form that was new and unexplored, there were no text books on screenwriting or experiences of others to refer to. There were no veterans of the field, only the pioneers. Those pioneers were men and women from all walks of life. Women, alongside men, made a valuable contribution into the development of the movie making in general and of screenwriting in particular.

Between 1895 – the invention by The Lumière brothers of the *cinematographe* motion system – and 1905, when their business was purchased by Gaumont company, the films, or '*photoplays*' as they were called back then, were mostly one-minute reel shots that required no script, as they were filmed on an ad hoc basis out on "the streets," picturing ordinary people minding their own

---

[98] Born in St Petersburg, Russia, Seraphima holds Bachelor of Science degree in English Language and English and American Literature. Being an innovator at heart, in 2006, she launched and ran the first digital only rich media magazine - Avantoure, - using Zinio technology. Having travelled the world and lived in such cities as London, New York, Moscow, Dubai, Geneva, Seraphima currently resides in Berlin. Since 2011, she has been focusing on writing/screenwriting, and independent creative projects. Her works include screenplays: Puzzled (in English), A Tricky Game (in English), and Golovolomka (in Russian); books: Golovolomka, Zadacha s neizvestnumi, and Zagadka Vostochnogo Expressa (all three books in Russian); and librettos for modern ballets: Christmas X 3, I'm Your Man (dedicated to Leonard Cohen), and A Night in Paris. www.seraphimabogomolova.com.

business. So, film directors were literally ad hoc life storytellers. All they needed was a camera, literally.

Among those early storytellers was one who laid the foundation for visual narrating and narrative filmmaking as opposed to filming just anything or anyone. This storyteller was a film director, Alice Guy Blanche (1873-1968), who worked for Gaumont in Paris, France.[99]

Alice Guy Blanche was the first female film director in the world. In her visual narratives, she experimented with sound synching, colour tinting, and special effects, all of which made her storytelling much more compelling and intriguing. By 1907, Alice Guy Blanche created over 1,000 films. The examples of her early narrative works are *Disappearing Act*[100] (1898), *At the Hypnotist*[101] (1898), as well as dance and travel short features such as *Serpentine Dance*[102] (1902), *Spain*[103] (1905).

The brief stories of this period of silent era can be compared to current TikTok videos – in just a minute an intriguing and captivating 'story' has to be told, or else, people will switch to something else. *"Brevity is the sister of talent"* as the Russian classic, Anton Chekov, once said. It still stands true.

As visual narrating continued to develop, a need for various story ideas and story synopsis had emerged. During the period of 1905 and 1915, these ideas came from the following sources – existing theatrical plays, published novels, and company-sponsored

---

[99] Films, Zeitgeist, "BE NATURAL: THE UNTOLD STORY OF ALICE GUY-BLACHÉ - official US trailer," YouTube (December 10, 2018)
https://www.youtube.com/watch?v=bPUJRtrp_EE&feature=youtu.be.
[100] Iconauta, "Alice Guy: Disappearing Act (1898)," YouTube (March 31, 2016)
https://www.youtube.com/watch?v=YrtSzfR4qNE&feature=youtu.be.
[101] Iconauta, "Alice Guy: At The Hypnotist (1898)," YouTube (March 15, 2016)
https://www.youtube.com/watch?v=IHNYjzM3hik.
[102] Rebmetpes9002, "Serpentine Dance by Lina Esbrard (1902) by Alice Guy," YouTube (July 29, 2011)
https://www.youtube.com/watch?v=hgbNYmQKWGk&feature=youtu.be.
[103] Productions, Going, Before, Change, "Spain (1905) - ALICE GUY BLACHE – Espagne," YouTube (April 26, 2012)
https://www.youtube.com/watch?v=pF0JiLzkEL4&feature=youtu.be.

contests advertised in popular fan magazines such as *Photoplay*. The readers of the fan magazines were mostly women who became winners of the early contests for the best story ideas that took the form of a few lines of text, a paragraph or a one-page plot summary.

Those early contests remind of the modern screenwriting competitions. The only difference is that back in 1910s all one needed to do is to reply to an advertisement with their story idea at a cost of a post stamp, whereas a contemporary aspiring screenwriter has to pay a certain fee for the privilege of supplying his or her synopsis or screenplay for a competition, often several competitions, which adds up to a significant sum of money. Win-win turned over 100 years into win-lose. The aspiring screenwriter being on a losing end.

At the period of 1905-1915 one could either be a free-lance writer working from home, or be a full-time employee of a film studio. Since the actual storytelling was happening on set with no scenario at hand, just a story idea or synopsis of it, writing was often combined with other roles - acting, assisting, or being a secretary to a film director. The on-set assistants and secretaries were called 'script girls'. They 'held the script', recording scenes, actions, dialogues, and shooting directions. They also wrote subtitles – explanations between some scenes, - as well as collected story ideas from the contests, and edited existing synopsises for film directors. The variety of the tasks performed allowed these women to later apply their on-set and off-set skills to developing scenarios.

A comment of an early scenario writer, Gene Gauntier (1885-1966) perfectly sums the skeletal nature of screenwriting process of the period:

"A poem, a picture, a short story, a scene from a current play, a headline in a newspaper. All was grist that came to my mill."[104]

---

[104] Bisplinghoff, Gretchen. "Gene Gauntier." In Jane Gaines, Radha Vatsal, and Monica Dall'Asta, eds. *Women Film Pioneers Project.* New York, NY: Columbia University Libraries, (2013)
https://wfpp.columbia.edu/pioneer/ccp-gene-gauntier/.

Some female writers who supplied story ideas and synopsis were teenagers, like Anita Loos[105] (1888-1981). She began her writing career by participating in magazine contests and caught the attention of a film director D.W. Griffith. Not aware of her age, D.W. Griffith fist mistook Anita's mother with whom she came for the interview for the writer he had sought after. This trend of teen story writers can be spotted in the current decade. Wattpad – an online publishing platform - offers opportunities for digitally sharing and publishing stories. Some just a few episodes long and some are finished works with millions of reads and large fan base such as a recent 'page to screen' adaptation of a Wattpad romance *Kissing Booth*[106] written in 2010 by then a teenager – Beth Reekles[107].

By the mid 1910s, the scenario started to take shape as something more than a story idea or synopsis implemented on set by a film director. And the need of a professional dramatist or a scenario writer working together with film directors had emerged.

Detailed scenarios, containing a title, the number of reels, a one paragraph synopsis, a cast, a list of props, and a detailed summary of each scene including its setting, character action, and maybe some dialogue, started to be produced. Scenarios of the time were based on theatrical plays, books, or were original creations by scenario writers.[108]

"In making plays from novels the rule is "Cut, cut, cut." In making photo dramas from novels the cry is "Put in more detail and action." And when you go to make a photo drama from the original every-day

---

[105] Ruvoli, JoAnne. "Anita Loos." In Jane Gaines, Radha Vatsal, and Monica Dall'Asta, eds. *Women Film Pioneers Project*. New York, NY: Columbia University Libraries, (2013) https://wfpp.columbia.edu/pioneer/ccp-anita-loos/.

[106] Reekles, "The Kissing Booth [SAMPLE] - Coming to Netflix May 11," Wattpad https://www.wattpad.com/story/203382-the-kissing-booth-sample-coming-to-netflix-may-11.

[107] Reekles, "Beth Reeks/@Reekles," Wattpad https://www.wattpad.com/user/Reekles.

[108] Peacoke, T., Leslie, Captain, "Hints on Photoplay Writing," N/A (1915) https://miro.medium.com/max/1400/1*t23NyqoS0SVXP-RiQXC14w.png

legitimate play, you have got to add material enough to double or treble the original manuscript. You have got to show all the things that the characters tell about in addition to showing all the things done on the stage, and then you have got to invent new things which happened before the play began and more things which happened after it was over. Then you may have enough." – Jesse L. Lasky, (*Photoplays of Tomorrow*, Photoplay magazine, June 1915).[109]

It is interesting to note that nowadays, movie making industry experiences similar challenges with finding story ideas for new releases. And as 100 years ago, producers and film directors turn to literature – classics, like Jane Austen, Louisa May Alcott, Charlotte Bronte, or contemporaries, like Helen Fielding, Suzanne Collins, Sara Jo Moyes, and Beth Reekles.

As scenario writing continued to develop, a guiding advice on the craft was also being provided. Both men and women offered their insights. Being the pioneers of scenario writing women were able to provide guidance in terms of plot conception, development, and its visualisation, and men were sticking to structural form of the story. Female scenario writers produced manuals, articles, and books for aspiring writers where they emphasized the importance of picturing the material - the essential element of storytelling for the screen.

An early photoplay dramatist, Catherine Carr (1880-1941), in her book *The Art of Photoplay Writing* (published by The Harris Jordan Co, N.Y., 1914) highlighted the importance of visualizing an action and even an emotion that will result in producing a human-interest story. In her interview for the Photoplay Author magazine when asked what her most reliable source of plots for photoplays are, she replied:

---

[109] Lasky, L, Jesse, "Photoplays of Tomorrow," Photoplay Magazine (1915) https://archive.org/stream/PhotoplayMagazineJune1915/Photoplay0615#page/n99/mode/2up.

"My best stories were found on little incidents of everyday life; incidents into which I injected motive and climax thereby turning them into actable and interesting stories."

June Mathis[110] (1887-1927), another female scenario writer, in *The Photoplay Journal* of 1917 stressed the importance of picturing:

"In your mind's eye you must visualize your plot, just as you would stand on a mountain top and gaze at beautiful scenery surrounding you. You must visualize your characters. You must see your characters."[111]

An invaluable piece of advice as visualising was something that many scenario writers of the time had a problem of mastering. The advice also stands true for some of the contemporary screenwriters. For, despite 100 years of movie making, they still forget it is for the screen they write and not for the reading.

Between 1908 and 1917 the increase in film length and the desire for well-made films with narrative fluidity prompted a shift from scenario script to continuity script. Continuity script was referred to as, "placing of the many scenes that go to make up the photoplay in a logical sequence so that the photoplay may run perfectly smoothly, without breaks and jumps which, otherwise, would have to be covered by wordy and explanatory subtitles." (*Photoplay* magazine, 1917)[112]

The developers of continuity scenarios who can be credited with the make-up of continuity as we know it today were a scenario writer and production editor, June Mathis (1887-1927), and a

---

[110] Wexman, Virginia Wright. "June Mathis." In Jane Gaines, Radha Vatsal, and Monica Dall'Asta, eds. *Women Film Pioneers Project*. New York, NY: Columbia University Libraries, (2013)
https://wfpp.columbia.edu/pioneer/ccp-june-mathis/.
[111] Mathis, June, "Pursuing A Motion Picture Plot," *The Photo-Play Journal* (1917)
https://archive.org/stream/photoplayjournal02lave#page/n331/mode/2up.
[112] "Sample of Continuity Scenario," (1917)
https://miro.medium.com/max/1400/1*NcfFmqXV8CxkkZOvR6mbbg.png.

producer and film director, Thomas Ince (1880-1924) at Metro film studios.

In continuity scenarios 'close-ups' and 'flash-backs' were frequently used as they were believed to support the idea that people like to see movement, emotions, and other people's faces as opposed to settings and landscapes on screen. The continuities also added the following to the scenario – film director, cast and actors, location, detailed *mis-en-scene*, intertitle placement, shooting schedule, budget and distribution plan.

Continuity scenarios emerged from the need to establish a structure for the production process before and during filming. For, with earlier scenarios-synopsises film directors often deviated from the plot and brought changes that were not always beneficial for the story logic and as such could influence financial gains of film studios. One of the mistakes that film makers of silent era wanted to avoid was having too many subtitles – text explaining what happens - for they believed that people went to movies to see pictures and not to read text on the screen.

The art of screenwriting was still new and even though there were many people wishing to write for photoplays they usually lacked experience writing for screen. One of the solutions was to employ dramatists – professional writers who knew about dramatic writing – and put them to work in a team with film directors for better result.

"The best directors realize now that to ensure a successful production there must be team work." (The Scenario Writer and The Director[113], *Photoplay* magazine, May 1917

---

[113] Peacoke, T., Leslie, Captain, "The Scenario Writer and The Director," *Photoplay Magazine* (1917)
https://archive.org/stream/photoplayvolume11112chic#page/643/mode/2up

Another solution was to nurture already existing talent that grew with the art itself – such as script girls, actors and actresses. They knew the technicalities and also had a pretty good idea of what was required and desired in scenarios.

As good continuity writers were hard to find, those who fit the bill were highly valued. Among early continuity writers were Clara Beranger[114] (1886-1956), Sada Cowan[115] (1882-1943), Beulah Marie Dix[116](1876-1970), and Bess Meredyth[117] (1890-1969).

"Now, there is nothing that so greatly delights a producing director's heart as to come across a strong original plot, told in a short synopsis, backed-up by a working scenario evolved in perfect and logical continuity – so that he can take the 'script in hand' and start to produce it, with safe knowledge that by following the script implicitly he will be making a production which will do him credit." – Jesse L. Lansky, (*Photoplay* magazine, April, 1917)

Sounds familiar? Well, movie making industry does not seem to have moved that far from this particular point in time.

As in 1910s, contemporary film makers seem to face and grapple with the same dilemmas of where to source story ideas and synopsis, how to relay stories on to screen in an enticing way, where to find screen writers who would understand filming

---

[114] Rossiter, Lori. "Clara Beranger." In Jane Gaines, Radha Vatsal, and Monica Dall'Asta, eds. *Women Film Pioneers Project*. New York, NY: Columbia University Libraries (2019) https://wfpp.columbia.edu/pioneer/clara-beranger/.

[115] Bajar, Daniela; Livia Bloom. "Sada Cowan." In Jane Gaines, Radha Vatsal, and Monica Dall'Asta, eds. *Women Film Pioneers Project*. New York, NY: Columbia University Libraries (2013) https://wfpp.columbia.edu/pioneer/ccp-sada-cowan/.

[116] Holliday, Wendy. "Beulah Marie Dix." In Jane Gaines, Radha Vatsal, and Monica Dall'Asta, eds. *Women Film Pioneers Project*. New York, NY: Columbia University Libraries (2013) https://wfpp.columbia.edu/pioneer/ccp-beulah-marie-dix/.

[117] Sturtevant, Victoria. "Bess Meredyth." In Jane Gaines, Radha Vatsal, and Monica Dall'Asta, eds. *Women Film Pioneers Project*. New York, NY: Columbia University Libraries (2013) https://wfpp.columbia.edu/pioneer/ccp-bess-meredyth/.

process as well as drama writing, and how to make film directors and screen writers work together as a team.

By the end of 1910s, filmmakers managed to solve in one way or the other challenges that faced them but when they thought they had finally nailed it, a new technological advancement had arrived – the sound – and turned everything upside down.

How the Symmetry and Aesthetics of *The Handmaid's Tale* Is Essential to Its Storytelling
by Zofia Wijaszka[118]

The Handmaid's Tale series based on Margaret Atwood's dystopian novel of the same name demands its audience's attention from the start. The narrative of Offred (Elisabeth Moss) and her female friends living in Gilead (Chicago in "before" time) is a brutal, incredibly violent tale. The series is skillfully crafted and well suited in today's society of the #MeToo movement, *Time's Up*, subject of abortion, and women's rights. In *The Handmaid's Tale*, females are deprived of their capability to talk, to write, to read, and are even deprived of their own names. For example, Offred was previously known by June before being owned by Fred Offred. In this world, Handmaids are continuously raped, beaten, shamed, and abused. The scenes are brutal and depressing to watch, as it's a strange feeling to view the scenes of rape while hearing the narrative of Offred, who reveals to you how to endure it.

The Handmaid's Tale has a storyline that hits close to home in contemporary and political culture but is also remarkably pleasing to the senses. It sounds crazy to type that, but it's true. Like some sort of cosmic peculiarity, our eyes experience a painful, cruel story, but at the same time, we witness beautiful images brimming with symmetry. Yet, the symmetry and colors play a crucial role in the storytelling of *The Handmaid's Tale*.

---

[118] Zofia resides in Los Angeles and is passionate about pop culture, film, and television. She graduated from the University of Wroclaw, Poland with a Bachelor's Degree in Journalism and Social Communication with Creative Writing. Her work revolves around women in television and film, but not only. She is a staff writer for First Showing and freelance writer for Awards Watch, Nerdist, Film Inquiry, In Their Own League, and more. Twitter – @thefilmnerdette.

Women in *The Handmaid's Tale* are the most essential piece of the story, this is not surprising as the series is mostly written and directed by women. Every scene brings a new feeling that is inverse to the one preceding. If you are a fan of the production or have a keen eye, you most likely noticed that there are four primary colors; red, green, black and grey. In this world, hierarchy is made clear by shades of clothing.

When examining tones in *The Handmaid's Tale*, it's easy to remark Handmaids and their scarlet gowns, blouses, and dresses. It symbolizes their fight — the blood they sacrifice each time they are raped, hit, or give birth. If one watches the episode, one can see that redness is continuously emphasized by its very own temperament and by the camera. But why this color is assigned to Handmaids? It may be because it's easily located, even in the distance. Handmaids try to escape the eternal torture over and again hence the shade making perfect sense, yet, it's the bravest, fiercest color in the world of *The Handmaid's Tale* palette — just like Handmaids.

During episode twelve of the newest season titled "Sacrifice", directed by Deniz Gamze Ergüven and written by Lynn Renee Maxcy, and Bruce Miller, the creators used a lot of natural light. It's mostly practiced in scenes with June sitting in her room and narrating or shots characterizing conversations between characters. The light comes from the window, rays of sunshine show the capacity of the interior. Many times, in mentioned scenes with June in her room, that sun rays seem to represent the contentment of the moment.

Colors and light like the ones in "Sacrifice" make a significant impact on the aesthetics of the series. The importance of geometry is highlighted every time Aunt Lydia (Ann Down) manages the gathering with her proteges, as Handmaids always compose the perfect squares or circles, divided by the paths for their Commanders and their wives. This is a repetitive sequence that ideally shows the symmetries that are used by *The Handmaid's Tale* directors and writers; it appeared in season three, episode "Household". In the scene, Commander Waterford makes a speech while the came is behind him (main photo). Viewers can see his blurred posture while the focus is held by the squares of Handmaids. The only thing you can see is red and white, feel the distress of women who don't know what will come next.

Alongside geometry, there is symmetry. Servants always stay in the perfect line, perfect circle, or any given shape. There is an "eye-pleasing" symmetry in the way Handmaids are presented; either when they're secretly meeting or see each other during shopping. The camera work altogether with the storyline and narrative makes a fascinating mix. When experiencing a heartbreaking moment in the plot, you are simply mesmerized by the craft of each angle, shot, and music selection. All of which is mostly the opposite of the present situation happening on the screen. These details wake ambivalent feelings. Making the art aspect of *The Handmaid's Tale* so vital to the plot — awakening viewers' perception to the fullest.

There is one particular scene showed at the beginning of each episode. The scene depicts Handmaids going down the staircase captured by a downward shot. The stairway is shaped like a fish – Ichthys. The symbol was used by Pagans as a fertility talisman in ancient times and appears in mythology, as well as in Christianity. The other one that roots deeply in my memory is June making the propaganda video in the latest season. The scene was reconstructed many times before by other productions, but at this moment, it seems to fit like a glove. The scene in reference is of the main character standing, angel wings behind her (the last picture). Television audiences recently saw a similar shot in *Game of Thrones* (with Daenerys and her dragon). Though this type of sequence was used many times before, it is still of incredible significance. June, with a serious face, demonstrates that she will fight until her last breath — leaving the audience to reflect on this image with no words — just feelings and emotions.

Another crucial element that adds to the aesthetics of the show is the camera work for *The Handmaid's Tale*; A zoom-in shot that portrays the character's expressions and emotions – frequently June.

There isn't one episode where this shot is not used, and is without a doubt, a signature of the Hulu series. The emotion, conflict, and utter disgust for the Gilead manifested on June's face became a symbol of rebellion and freedom. Together with Offred's narrative (often with profanities and a grand soundtrack), the shot creates a token, metaphor —women empowerment depicted by one face. This is enhanced by Elisabeth Moss' splendid acting. Similar angles are also used for Yvonne Strahovski who portrays Serena Joy Waterford — a woman who seems to loathe other women, yet, becomes a friend, mother, and traitor. Strahovski solitary portrays each one of those characteristics just by acting with her facial highlights.

The variety of music in Bruce Mille's series will satisfy any viewer. The soundtrack is composed by Adam Taylor. However we can also catch hits like: "I Don't Like Mondays" by The Boomtown Rats, "You Make Me Feel Like Dancing" by Leo Sayer, and Belinda Carlisle's "Heaven Is a Place On Earth". The last one plays during a pivotal scene at the hospital (episode "Heroic" from season three). The scene consists of June losing her sanity as a patient. As the hours and days blur into one, the life machine starts beeping in the rhythm of "Heaven is A Place On Earth". It's one of the most memorable scenes from the latest season. *The Handmaid's Tale* is the barbarous story of the end of women's rights, but the 80s inspired soundtrack evokes feelings of dancing. Like the case of other aspects mentioned above, this creates a sense of ambivalence while watching the series. Perhaps that is the goal — diverse emotions — but that's a question for the creator.

There are similar scenes that you can fall in love with, but it's hard to see in writing — you simply have to see it. Although the main subject of *The Handmaid's Tale* is controversial, perception by the senses takes power as well. All these components described combines into one picture that harmonizes perfectly with the acting. As noted, a good storyline is always essential, but the way the product is made is crucial too. Everyone should experience these ambivalent yet so pleasing emotions — and of course, hear Moira (Samira Wiley) say:

Praised be, bitch!

The Brilliance of Zack Snyder's DC Universe

by Christopher Pierznik[119]

His superhero films, full of complex characters, deep symbolism, and faithfulness to the comics, are unlike anything ever seen before — and possibly ever again.

"You and we know that it is generally just the best and most valuable things that do not find their echo immediately."
—Kurt Woolf, in a letter to Franz Kafka

I. The Beginning

We are living in the age of the comic book film.

The highest-grossing film franchise of all time is the Marvel Cinematic Universe (MCU). Since its inception in 2008, the franchise has released nineteen movies that have grossed $15 billion globally (and counting) and, considering its most recent films, *Black Panther* and *Avengers: Infinity War*, shattered box office records, it does not appear to be slowing down any time soon.

Yet while Marvel is a record-breaking worldwide juggernaut, it was actually their rival, DC Comics — through Warner Bros. — that introduced the superhero film in 1978 with *Superman*. With the tagline "You'll believe a man can fly," the black-and-white image of George Reeves jumping out of a window was replaced by

---

[119] Christopher Pierznik is the author of 9 books and has contributed to numerous websites and publications on a variety of topics including music, sports, TV, movies, personal finance, parenthood, and life. By day, he works in analytics and lives in northern New Jersey with his family. His work can be found at ChristopherPierznik.com.

Christopher Reeve and Richard Donner's genre-defining approach that made it look as if Kal-El really were flying over Metropolis.

In the decades that followed, as Marvel teetered on the verge of bankruptcy, WB kept churning out films based on DC Comics, mostly based on Batman and Superman — from the sequels of that original *Superman*, to the Tim Burton and Joel Schumacher Batman series, to Bryan Singer's *Superman Returns*, all the way to Christopher Nolan's *The Dark Knight* trilogy, which concluded in 2012 — but also Steel, Catwoman, Constantine, V for Vendetta, Watchmen, Green Lantern, and others. Yet, while the characters often crossed over in the comics and even the animated shows, the films stood alone. No DC superheroes interacted with any others outside of their immediate realm on the big screen.

In May, 2008, Marvel Studios released *Iron Man* and followed it up with *The Incredible Hulk* a month later, thus kicking off the Marvel Cinematic Universe, a series of films with overlapping characters and small plots within one large, overarching plot, all of it overseen by one person: Kevin Feige. The enormous — and enduring — success of the MCU made a shared universe a dream of every studio, most especially Marvel's lifelong rival.

II. Birth of a Universe

The MCU would go on to change Hollywood forever, but it didn't happen overnight. In fact, although Marvel released its first two films in 2008, neither became the biggest superhero film of 2008. That honor belonged to *The Dark Knight*, the second installment of Christopher Nolan's Batman series that would become the highest-grossing film of the year, both domestically and worldwide (*Iron Man* would finish second in North America and eighth globally).[120]

---

[120] "2008 in Film – Highest-grossing films of 2008," Wikipedia https://en.wikipedia.org/wiki/2008_in_film.

Still, Nolan's Batman existed in a world all his own, driven to don the cape and cowl because of what Gotham had become — and what it had made him. So, there would be no other heroes in Nolan's universe, meaning that although they had a decades-long head start, Warner Bros. was suddenly behind, having allowed Marvel to gain an even stronger foothold in the world of comic book films.

That same summer, Warner Bros. executives, seeing how Batman (and The Incredible Hulk) could be successfully rebooted, immediately went to work on reviving the crown jewel of DC Comics: Superman. Following the release of *The Dark Knight*, Nolan and writer David S. Goyer were discussing story ideas for a third Batman film when Goyer said he knew how to make a modern Superman film. "Nolan said he took that idea and pitched it to Warner Bros., and the studio got excited, too. 'But it's not something for me to direct,' he added. 'It's something we were just trying to put together a vision for, and then find the right person to take it forward.'"[121]

Who was that right person?

Zack Snyder.

Snyder had already brought a comic to the big screen with *300* in 2006 and again three years later with *Watchmen*. His style was visual, the shots akin to a splash page. Both films look like the graphic novels of Frank Miller and Alan Moore came to life.

It wasn't only the costumes or the settings. Even the way he films his shots — which most critics despise — make the films feel like a real-world illustration.[122]

---

[121] "Christopher Nolan on Batman and Superman," *SuperheroHype* (June 4, 2010) https://www.superherohype.com/news/102090-christopher-nolan-on-batman-and-superman#MECSt2Eik2FxkDr7.99.

[122] Bunch, Sonny. "The Zack Snyder Era of Superhero Movies Is Over. You Should Be Sorry to See it Go," *The Washington Post* (February 20, 2018) https://www.washingtonpost.com/news/act-four/wp/2018/02/20/the-zack-snyder-era-of-superhero-movies-is-over-you-should-be-sorry-to-see-it-go/?noredirect=on.

The reason Snyder's previous comic-book adaptations, *300* and *Watchmen*, had worked was that the speed-ramping effect he so loved — in which he slowed down the action and sped it back up as the camera drifted along, a spectator to carnage — perfectly mimicked the experience of reading a comic book. You see a frame and then another frame, but not what happens between them. Speeding up, then slowing down, suggests how the eye flits across the page, going from one act of violence to another.

Films, of course, are not solely a visual medium. There is also storytelling, plot, pacing and, most of all, character development. Comic book heroes and villains are, by their very nature, not like anyone else and cannot be presented as such. Yet, at the same time, a real effort was made for films to treat these characters and the worlds in which they inhabit seriously. This was certainly true for Christopher Nolan, who went to great lengths to explain how Bruce Wayne could become Batman in a real world.

Snyder had a similar view and was determined to bring a realistic approach to the material — presumably that is what led Nolan to tap him to bring a plausible Kal-El to the screen. As Nolan said of Snyder:

> *"Zack has an innate aptitude for dealing with superheroes as real characters. That was what a new approach to Superman required. He understands the power of iconic images, but he also understands the people behind them."*[123]

Finally, after several uninspiring sequels, decades of dormancy, and a false restart, Superman would be returning to theaters and, in the process, would be introducing the DC Extended Universe (DCEU).

---

[123] Itzkoff, Dave. "Alien, Yet Familiar," *The New York Times* (May 22, 2013) https://www.nytimes.com/2013/05/26/movies/man-of-steel-aims-to-make-superman-relevant-again.html.

III. A Super Vision

What if Superman existed in our current reality? How would the world react to a literal illegal alien — the ultimate immigrant[124] — with godlike abilities? And how would he, in turn, react to the world?

That is the idea that underpins *Man of Steel*, the *Batman Begins* version of Superman that Snyder directed and Nolan "godfathered."[125] While it is a solo origin story, it does include easter eggs that hint at the larger DCEU, including a reference to Booster Gold and a quick shot of a Wayne Enterprises satellite.[126]

In fact, *Man of Steel* was planned as the opening chapter of a five-chapter story (much like a limited comic run)[127] that was going to be "epic, grand, emotional, joyful and unforgettable"[128] with *Batman v Superman: Dawn of Justice* acting as chapter two, the start of that film actually overlapping with the ending of *Man of Steel*. While the DCEU Superman is a confused, burdened messiah, Batman has clear allusions to Frank Miller's seminal *The Dark Knight Returns*. Frustrated and cynical after twenty years of trying to overcome a Sisyphean task — "Criminals are like weeds, Alfred; pull one up, another grows in its place" — and haunted by the death of not only his parents, but also Robin, he has lost his moral compass. He sees Superman as the ultimate global

---

[124] Farooqi, Sheraz. "The Ultimate Immigrant Story: Zack Snyder's Superman," *Geeks Of Color* (August 17, 2017)
https://geeksofcolor.co/2017/08/17/the-ultimate-immigrant-story-zack-snyders-superman/.
[125] Wigler, Josh. "Christopher Nolan to 'Mentor' New Superman Movies, Unlikely to Direct," *MTV* (February 9, 2010)
http://www.mtv.com/news/2596025/christopher-nolan-to-mentor-new-superman-movies-unlikely-to-direct/
[126] Chitwood, Adam. "Man of Steel Easter Eggs and DC Comics References You May Have Missed," *Collider* (June 17, 2013)
https://collider.com/man-of-steel-easter-eggs/.
[127] Olivia, Jay, [@jayolivia1], Twitter (April 21, 2018)
https://twitter.com/jayoliva1/status/987858571357388800.
[128] Olivia, Jay, [@jayolivia1], Twitter (May 16, 2018)
https://twitter.com/jayoliva1/status/996961088120930304.

threat and decides that taking out Gotham street punks pales in comparison to saving the world.

BvS was just another building block in Sndyer's universe creation, which would have continued with the optimistic and redemptive *Justice League*. He had very bold plans. Even those that despise Snyder's work could never accuse him of not bringing a grand vision to the DCEU:

"More than a house style, however, Snyder oversaw a house ethos. And it's here that the recent spate of DC films — as wildly uneven as they were, as messy as they could be purely in terms of storytelling — has always been more consistent, and more interesting, than their counterparts at Marvel. Consider Tony Stark (Robert Downey Jr.), the key to the MCU's success. He is wildly erratic as a character, swinging from libertarian privatizer of peacekeeping to statist global governance proponent to mad genius tinkering with godhood to father figure aiding a kid in need, depending on what the movie he happens to be in needs him to do to keep the action moving. He's a plot device, not a person. There's a unity of vision to the Snyder-led DC movies that is simply lacking over at Marvel."[129]

Regardless of how one feels about Snyder's work, no one can ever accuse it of not being ambitious.[130] However, ambition often means eschewing safety and that can be alienating or even upsetting to those that want something comfortable and expected. He was taking a different approach to the genre and viewing these characters in completely new ways on screen and completely subverting expectations.

---

[129] Bunch, Sonny, "The Zack Snyder Era of Superhero Movies Is Over. You Should Be Sorry to See it Go," *The Washington Post* (February 20, 2018)
https://www.washingtonpost.com/news/act-four/wp/2018/02/20/the-zack-snyder-era-of-superhero-movies-is-over-you-should-be-sorry-to-see-it-go/?noredirect=on.
[130] Naahar, Rohan, "In Defence of the DCEU: Why the Justice League Universe Is More Ambitious than the Avengers," *HindustanTimes* (November 16, 2017)
https://www.hindustantimes.com/hollywood/in-defence-of-the-dceu-why-the-justice-league-universe-is-more-ambitious-than-the-avengers/story-AMEWwm141gGuq635W-WARqK.html.

"That's what Snyder was doing, and he envisioned something ambitious and bold — an entire superhero cinematic approach that starts off by positing a new type world in which superhero exist, deconstructing the genre itself right in front of our eyes and building something unlike any we'd seen before in superhero cinema. The genre already existed and had dozens of entries by this point, so Snyder realized it wasn't enough to start off with just another template-style approach which would be deconstructed later — doing it from the outset, with the knowledge audiences already have a built-in map of the genre and of the most famous of these characters, and from the outset challenging all of their assumptions so this otherwise familiar genre and familiar set of characters could not be taken for granted, and instead would surprise us time and again, was the goal."[131] When *Batman v Superman* was screened for Warner Bros. executives, they loved it so much that they gave it a standing ovation and immediately decided that they wanted to Ben Affleck to keep portraying the Caped Crusader for the foreseeable future.[132]

The good feelings would not last long, however. Few would understand, much less appreciate, that vision and, as a result, he was never given the opportunity to see it through to completion.

IV. The Reactions – and the Reactions to Those Reactions

Upon its release, *Man of Steel* received mixed reviews with much of the criticism focused on the changes made to the

---

[131] Hughes, Mark, "What Zack Snyder's DCEU Was Really All About, And Why So Many People Rejected It," *Forbes* (January 30, 2018) https://www.forbes.com/sites/markhughes/2018/01/30/what-zack-snyders-dceu-was-really-all-about-and-why-so-many-people-rejected-it/#1afa1fed5f29.
[132] Steinbeiser, Andrew, "Rumor Batman v Superman Screening Gets Standing Ovation, Affleck Getting Long Term Deal," *ComicBook* (September 6, 2017) https://comicbook.com/news/batman-v-superman-screening-gets-standing-ovation-affleck-gettin/.

Superman mythos — from the suit to his actions. Many found it to be un-Superman-like for him to be so focused on stopping General Zod that he (a) did not once stop to consider how their fight was decimating much of Metropolis and (b) ended his life.

Snyder knew what he was doing. He said, "that killing Zod was part of the learning curve that would transform a scared and confused kid into the Superman fans know and love by the end of the *Justice League* films." He was also quite cognizant of the fact that the destruction of Metropolis and the resulting collateral damage would be a sore spot for some, namely those that have a very narrow view of what Superman is and should be, and that's why it is shown from the perspective of the people at the start of *BvS* and is really the point on which the entire plot is based.

While reviews for *Man of Steel* fell in the middle — 55% on Rotten Tomatoes vs. 75% audience score — *Batman v Superman: Dawn of Justice* was pilloried, resulting in an avalanche of gleefully nasty reviews and an aggregate score of 27% (though a 63% audience score).[133] A pattern emerged: "Fan reception to Man of Steel was much warmer than the critical reception — something that would become a recurring motif for the DC films."[134] BvS is almost certainly the most divisive superhero film of all time:

"While it was critically savaged, *Batman v Superman* has a deeply devoted following who adore it for its dark deconstruction of DC's two biggest icons. Indeed, it's hard not to wonder if *Batman v Superman* would have been more warmly received in 2017; while *Wonder Woman* is a ray of light in a dark world, *Batman v Superman* embraces that darkness with a level of glee that borders on nihilism. That level of cynicism was off putting

---

[133] DC Extended Universe Features, *RottenTomatoes* (N/A) https://www.rottentomatoes.com/franchise/dc_comics.
[134] Burlingame, Russ, "Batman v Superman Art Director Corrects Hitman Producer's 'Revisionist History'," *ComicBook* (May 1, 2018) https://comicbook.com/dc/news/batman-v-superman-art-director-corrects-hitman-producers-revisio/.

for most viewers in early 2016, and yet it feels oddly prescient at the tail end of 2017, predicting the chaotic forces that would come to dominate real world events soon after its release."[135]

It's weird that a film that made nearly $900 million and boasts both iconic American characters and multiple Academy Award-nominated actors could be a cult classic, but that is what *BvS* has become, largely because of the beating it took at the hands of critics. Its fans argue that it is one of the most misunderstood films in recent years — or ever[136] — and feel as if the professional reviewers had a clear bias, that their reactions were more personal than professional, as if Zack Snyder's style and approach were reprehensible and it was impossible that anyone would prefer or enjoy it:

"The quick responses, sadly, showed how clearly the dislike, scorn, and negative feedback for anything *Batman v Superman*, or indeed DC or Snyder-related wasn't coming from a critical source. Those who disliked the film weren't part of a homogeneous group, but for the most prominent voices, it wasn't enough to simply make their opinion that Snyder's work was objectively bad, creatively bankrupt, or terribly misguided known. Going a step further, anyone who *questioned* that consensus, highlighted overlooked elements, or sought to *engage* with the work was foolish, pitiably zealous, and deserving of less than respectful response. There is simply no grey area: that response or attitude is NOT a critical one, in the spirit of the word or philosophy. As time passed, many online personalities or pundits who considered themselves 'critics' took this same stance against the idea of criticism as a conversation and investigation, outright refusing to question, consider, or respectfully engage with opposing opinions."[137]

---

[135] Stowe, Dusty, "Justice League Should Have Been More Like Batman v Superman," *ScreenRant* (November 26, 2017)
https://screenrant.com/justice-league-too-safe-batman-v-superman/.

[136] Pitviper, "Batman v Superman: The Most Misunderstood Film Ever," *Medium* (May 20, 2017)
https://medium.com/@pitviper1157/batman-v-superman-the-most-misunderstood-film-ever-a90bb99cbe76.

[137] Dyce, Andrew, "Batman v Superman Fans Have Shown Where 'Critics' Failed," *ScreenRant* (April 24, 2018)
https://screenrant.com/batman-v-superman-critics-failed-snyder-fans/2/.

There were a multitude of criticisms lobbed at Snyder's first two DCEU films (as well as the universe's third, *Suicide Squad*, which he executive produced), but perhaps the most common was that they were dour, joyless affairs. Perhaps I loved them because I've long been annoyed with happy Hollywood endings. While some watch films for an escape, there are those of us that want to see the real world reflected back at them through a certain lens and the seriousness is actually what makes the films realistic and believable:

> *"The world is cynical, skeptical, and jaded. War, poverty, violence, hatred — these are the daily realities for so many people, and even those in positions of so-called power realize how helpless they are to stop most of it. Lex Luthor's remark about a person with knowledge being smart enough to realize they are powerless in the world is a crucial hint into his own psyche and how the scars of this lesson were beaten into him from a young age, for example. He articulates a truth, a knowledge about the powerlessness of mankind in the face of our own destructive impulses, and that we pretend toward power and knowledge to shield ourselves from those realities."*[138]

Moreover, despite what many would have you believe, both *Man of Steel* and *Batman v Superman* had moments of levity and humor, though they were delivered in a dry, offhanded way. *BvS* stands as the low point of the multifilm arc, the nadir for the characters from which they can recover and ultimately find salvation. It is not unlike any other second act or middle part of a series (much like *The Empire Strikes Back* or *Infinity War*).

Yet rather than judge the films on what they were or what they were trying to do, a large swath of people lambasted them

---

[138] Hughes, Mark, "Zack Snyder Loves Superman, And Batman v Superman Proves It," *Forbes* (March 29, 2016)
https://www.forbes.com/sites/markhughes/2016/03/29/zack-snyder-loves-superman-and-batman-v-superman-proves-it/#c8f7e35c64bb.

because they were not what they wanted or expected — and that is one area in which DC's crossover legacy is a hindrance. For many, Christopher Reeve is the ultimate Superman and the way the character was portrayed was the only proper way to do so, meaning that any variations will immediately be scrutinized if not completely dismissed. The same is even more true for Batman — everyone has their own favorite version of the Dark Knight, whether it is Adam West or Michael Keaton or Christian Bale, so it is already an uphill battle. Some of those films and performances entered the public consciousness and became iconic, meaning that any changes or updates are immediately risky. That is one reason why Jesse Eisenberg's Lex Luthor was, like the film itself, so divisive.[139]

One character, however, was not.

Perhaps at least part of the reason Wonder Woman's appearance was so warmly embraced was because there had never before been a live-action film version to which audiences would measure it. That's something that has benefited Marvel. Not only were they first with their shared universe, but it was also almost a completely blank slate. Since their most popular characters had been optioned by other studios, they needed to look deeper into the roster to create their universe. There had never before been a big screen adaptation for Iron Man or Thor, let alone the Guardians of the Galaxy, so there were no previously held notions or comparisons weighing them down:

> *"Putting aside all of the hostility and simplistic assertions rooted in narrow attitudes and silly personal resentments, I think the biggest*

---

[139] Stowe, Dusty, "15 Reasons Jesse Eisenberg's Lex Luthor Is the BEST Version," *ScreenRant* (July 10, 2017)
https://screenrant.com/jesse-eisenberg-lex-luthor-best-version-batman-v-superman-adaptation/.

problem has been an approach that often contradicts the prevailing mainstream public impressions and expectations for several of the central characters — specifically, Superman, and to a lesser extent Batman."[140]

Many casual fans do not understand the different machinations of these characters and simply want more of the same. As such, Snyder had been criticized for being *too* faithful to the source material.[141] Imagine such a statement considering it wasn't that long ago in a film that Batman not only pulled out a Bat credit card, but did so to purchase a woman. Snyder himself has said, "I love the characters, and maybe to a fault sometimes, I dork out on the hardcore aspects of the comic books." Alas, many casual fans and most critics do not. His faithfulness to the comics is astounding, but the general public doesn't know the *Injustice: Gods Among Us* storyline or the intricacies of the New 52 and instead only know that Superman changes in a phone booth (which no longer exist) or Batman never uses a gun (despite the fact that he did it numerous times in the comics). This iteration of the characters was unfamiliar to the larger public:

"Batman v Superman showcases a version of the Caped Crusader that wide audiences had never really seen; not simply a Batman who is losing his fight against crime, but who has, for all intents and purposes, already lost. Batman, generally portrayed as the smartest DC hero, acts in brash, shortsighted ways, as he's so blinded by the paranoia and fear that he fought against for so many years. He exists in a bubble of his own misery and cynicism, convinced the world is spinning out of control as the emergence of godlike beings push his feelings of helplessness into overdrive."[142]

---

[140] Hughes, Mark, "What Zack Snyder's DCEU Was Really All About, And Why So Many People Rejected It," *Forbes* (January 30, 2018) https://www.forbes.com/sites/markhughes/2018/01/30/what-zack-snyders-dceu-was-really-all-about-and-why-so-many-people-rejected-it/#1afa1fed5f29.

[141] Owen, Paul. "Watchmen Is Too Faithful to Alan Moore's Book," *The Guardian* (July 22, 2009) https://www.theguardian.com/film/filmblog/2009/jul/22/watchmen-book-film-alan-moore.

[142] Stowe, Dusty, "Justice League Should Have Been More Like Batman v Superman," *ScreenRant* (November 26, 2017) https://screenrant.com/justice-league-too-safe-batman-v-superman/.

Justice League was always meant to be more optimistic. A superhero team-up as well as a redemption story, it was always going to have a lighter tone than the previous films because that is the arc of the story. "*Man of Steel* was Zack Snyder's first Superman movie. Its direct sequel, *Batman v Superman* introduced the Dark Knight to hold Superman accountable for the prior film. And finally, the events of *both* previous films all led to *Justice League* — uniting DC's biggest heroes as the thematic and logical conclusion, meant to signal the arrival of a brighter future (that was the plan, anyway)."[143]

The negative, vitriolic reactions to *BvS* led Warner Bros. executives to panic and abandon that plan. The studio took the unusual step to fly critics in to see how much more upbeat the next film would be and that the character deconstruction would be kept to a minimum. WB went to great lengths to ensure that this time would be different. They probably didn't realize just *how* different.

V. Justice Denied

The rumors started almost immediately. The early cut of *Justice League* was "unwatchable"[144] and Snyder had "opted out"[145] of directing any future films. These leaks seemed like plants, however, and considering Snyder's love for the source material and all of the universe building he had done, it seemed unlikely he would just walk away halfway through.

---

[143] Dyce, Andrew, "The DC Movie Universe Is Worse Without Zack Snyder," *ScreenRant* (November 27, 2017)
https://screenrant.com/zack-snyder-dceu-movie-universe-future/2/.
[144] Stowe, Dusty, "Rumor Patrol: Justice League Was 'Unwatchable' Before Reshoots," *ScreenRant* (August 12, 2017)
https://screenrant.com/rumor-justice-league-unwatchable-reshoots-zack-snyder-joss-whedon/.
[145] Hadden, James, "Rumor: Zack Snyder Has Opted Out of Directing Justice League 2; Won't Return for Man of Steel 2," *ScreenGeek* (August 27, 2016)
https://www.screengeek.net/2016/08/27/rumor-zack-snyder-opted-out-directing-justice-league-2-wont-return-for-man-steel-2/.

Of course, he would leave eventually. Upon the tragic news of his daughter's suicide, it was announced that Snyder was stepping down from *Justice League* and Joss Whedon, writer/director of the first *Avengers* films, whom Snyder had supposedly brought on to help with reshoots, would simply handle the finishing touches.

Slowly, however, more information began to leak out and there were numerous reports that Snyder had actually been fired[146] long before his exit had been announced. Despite the fact that studies have proven that Rotten Tomatoes scores do not impact box office figures[147], WB executives had had enough of the negative press and disappointing returns and chose to go in a completely new direction. However, the company micromanaged the film even more than initially thought[148] and decreed a running time of less than two hours. Still, despite their demands, they refused to push back the release date. Why? The answer, as always, is money:

> *"One executive told The Wrap Tsujihara and Emmerich 'wanted to preserve their bonuses they would be paid before the merger,' and were worried that 'if they pushed the movie, then their bonuses would have been pushed to the following year and they might not still be at the studio.'"*[149]

As a result, *Justice League* ended up as a rushed Frankenstein of a film with two contrasting styles mashed together that resulted

---

[146] Brail, Nathaniel, "Rumor: Zack Snyder Was Fired From Justice League Over a Year Ago," *HeroicHollywood* (February 10, 2018)
https://heroichollywood.com/zack-snyder-fired-justice-league-year/.

[147] Wallenstein, Andrew, "Rotten Tomatoes Scores Don't Impact Box Office, Study Finds," *Variety* (September 11, 2017)
https://variety.com/2017/film/news/rotten-tomatoes-scores-dont-impact-box-office-study-finds-1202554546/.

[148] Robinson, Joanna, "Justice League Was Apparently Micromanaged Even More Than We Thought," *VanityFair* (November 24, 2017)
https://www.vanityfair.com/hollywood/2017/11/justice-league-edits-joss-whedon-micromanaged-zack-snyder.

[149] Gonzalez, Umberto and Molloy, Tim, "How Justice League Became a 'Frankenstein' (Exclusive)," *TheWrap* (November 29, 2017)
https://www.thewrap.com/justice-league-zack-snyder-batman-v-superman-wonder-woman/.

in a disjointed mess and clearly delineated the two competing factions of those that watch DCEU films. Most critics praised Whedon's parts and thought they should have been the entirety of the film — "much of what does work in *Justice League* feels as if it can be more easily associated with Whedon instead of director Snyder."[150]

Some outlets even pointed to the final shot of Clark ripping open his shirt to reveal the Superman logo — an iconic American image — as proof that Whedon could have made a brilliant *Justice League* on his own. After all, that scene is very bright and hopeful, no way Zack Snyder could have shot that.

Actually, he *did* shoot it.

While the critical consensus was that Whedon was thankfully taking the franchise in a new direction, others — such as yours truly — felt robbed because Snyder's film was mutilated, his vision tarnished, and unnecessary goofy sitcom-style jokes were crammed into it while Junkie XL's score was abandoned in favor of the safe choice, Danny Elfman. The reshoots were not minor, as everyone initially claimed. Rather, they "drastically altered the final film."[151]

Some of the best images (including those used to promote the film) were nowhere to be found, including classic Snyder shots that look as if they were ripped straight out of a graphic novel.

So much was cut out. The black Superman suit. Cyborg's entire backstory. Kal-El's proper resurrection. Entire characters scrapped or curtailed mightily. Long-term plans for *Justice League 2* or perhaps even a trilogy. Tying up of loose threads. Superman's lip (which Snyder even mocked on social media). All of it — gone.

---

[150] Spiegel, Josh, "Did Justice League Learn Anything from Avengers?," *The Hollywood Reporter* (November 19, 2017)
https://www.hollywoodreporter.com/heat-vision/justice-league-did-joss-whedons-avengers-teach-movie-anything-1059198.
[151] Evangelista, Chris, "These Justice League Reshoots Drastically Altered the Final Film," SlashFilm (November 20, 2017)
https://www.slashfilm.com/these-justice-league-reshoots-drastically-altered-the-final-film/.

The lighter tone and shorter run time could not overcome the drama surrounding production. The edicts did not work and Justice League (or "Josstice League") failed to attract the mainstream audience, becoming the lowest-grossing DCEU film[152] and creating a shakeup at WB while Snyder fans dreamed of one day seeing the director's original film. It's ironic that many of those that fired Snyder found themselves out of a job.[153]

Even before *Man of Steel*, Snyder was already known for dark tones and complex plots with films that were at their best when presented in longer, director's cut forms. Presumably, they knew that's what he would bring to the DC universe. If you're going to hire him, why change his trilogy (or pentalogy) 85% of the way through the process? *Suicide Squad* further references the murder of Robin and Justice League would have featured the Anti-Life Equation.[154] Why not let him pay all of this off?

"If they'd let Snyder finish the job, we'd have ended up with another polarizing film with a clear identity, instead of this freakish personality-free hybrid. Then, when the film disappointed at the box office Snyder could have taken the fall and the DC Extended Universe could be handed over to someone else. Because when I watched Justice League, I wasn't thinking about how Snyder screwed this up. I was thinking that the execs at Warner Bros. have no idea what they're doing. Not if they think Justice League is a movie anyone wants to ever sit through again."[155]

---

[152] Baker-Whitelaw, Gavia, "Justice League Lost Warner Bros. a Whole Lot of Money," *DailyDot* (March 20, 2018)
https://www.dailydot.com/parsec/justice-league-box-office-flop/.
[153] Kaye, Ben, "DC Films Is Firing Pretty Much Everyone Responsible for Disastrous Justice League Move," ConsequenceOfSound (December 8, 2017)
https://consequenceofsound.net/2017/12/dc-films-is-firing-pretty-much-everyone-responsible-for-disastrous-justice-league-movie/.
[154] Dyce, Andrew, "Zack Snyder Teases Anti-Life Equation in Justice League Flashback?," *ScreenRant* (March 21, 2018)
https://screenrant.com/justice-league-anti-life-equation-zack-snyder/.
[155] Houvouras, Anghus, "Why Warner Bros. Should Have Left Zack Snyder's DCEU Alone," *FlickeringMyth* (December 26, 2017)
https://www.flickeringmyth.com/2017/12/why-warner-bros-should-have-left-zack-snyder-dceu-alone/.

At that point, you could reboot using the *Flashpoint* storyline (which seems like was already the plan considering Flash's appearance to Bruce in *BvS* and Cyborg taking center stage in many of the group shots). At least then you'd keep your rabid core audience.

I'm not exaggerating or being hyperbolic when I say *BvS* was truly a transformative movie-going experience for me (even before the expanded "Ultimate Edition"). Everyone has one, or a few, films they saw in the theater that they couldn't stop thinking or talking about — *Batman v Superman* was that film for me.

Man of Steel and *Batman v Superman* are films that stay with you long after watching them, regardless of how you feel about them. *BvS* stirred up a tornado of emotions on both sides — it's been more than two years since it was released and people are still yelling at each other over it — while *Justice League* came and went with a shrug.

Rather than continuing to push the envelope, WB decided to try to play it safe in an attempt to thread the needle and failed:

"And yet Justice League unquestionably lacks a certain spark that Batman V Superman has in spades. Batman V Superman feels dangerous — the work of an artist pushing at the boundaries of his genre in an attempt to say something new about these characters who have been part of the American lexicon for almost eight decades...It's difficult to imagine anyone discussing Justice League with that level of fervor even a month from now..." [156]

They spent far more money to change the film and the box office receipts were actually worse. (Anecdotally, I saw *BvS* twice in the theater but didn't see *Justice League* until it was available for home viewing because the studio meddling kept me away.)

---

[156] Stowe, Dusty, "Justice League Should Have Been More Like Batman v Superman," *ScreenRant* (November 26, 2017).
https://screenrant.com/justice-league-too-safe-batman-v-superman/.

In short, it didn't work and now, instead of a film that would have probably been loved — and, yes, derided — by many, it's a film that was milquetoast and immediately forgotten. It failed to attract the general public while pissing off the relatively small but extremely loud and loyal core fans to the point that they were calling the CEO of Warner Bros. the best film villain of the year and more than 200,000 people signing petitions and demanding to #ReleaseTheSnyderCut until it finally happened.

It isn't only the fans. Ray Fisher, who played Cyborg, has left cryptic messages that seem to point to his disappointment with how *Justice League* turned out[157] while Ciaran Hinds, who portrayed Steppenwolf, actually vocalized that he prefers the Snyder Cut: "That wasn't the movie I worked so hard on. We hope the director's cut comes out because it was better than the movie in the theaters."[158] Later, Jason Momoa said he was "obsessed" with the idea of the Snyder Cut.[159]

Snyder's first two efforts are still being debated and discussed because they resonated and that is a direct result of the director's ambitious plans: "Looking back at every step along the way, the evidence — and filmmakers — say DC's success (with average box office of $775M per film) has more to do with Zack Snyder's vision than his critics would ever admit. And judging by the reception to *Justice League*, WB's attempt to grab the reins back has left more questions than answers."[160]

---

[157] Begley, Chris, "Zack Snyder and Ray Fisher Share Photos from Deleted Justice League Scene," *Batman-News* (March 21, 2018) https://batman-news.com/2018/03/31/zack-snyder-and-ray-fisher-share-photos-from-deleted-justice-league-scene/.

[158] "JL's Steppenwolf Ciaran Hinds Says That the Snyder Cut Is Better Than the Theatrical Cut," *CinemaCure* (February 13, 2018) https://cinemacure.wordpress.com/2018/02/13/jls-steppenwolf-ciaran-hinds-says-that-the-snyder-cut-is-better-than-the-theatrical-cut/.

[159] *MTV News*,[@MTVNEWS], Twitter (December 7, 2018) https://twitter.com/MTVNEWS/status/1071159918126755840.

[160] Dyce, Andrew, "The DC Movie Universe Is Worse Without Zack Snyder," *ScreenRant* (November 27, 2017) https://screenrant.com/zack-snyder-dceu-movie-universe-future/.

VI. References, Allusions, Symbolism & Iconopraphy

While so many films come and go, Zack Snyder's DCEU efforts continue to be topics of conversation. Though they were not well-received initially, it appears that both time and multiple viewings have led to a greater appreciation and understanding of *Man of Steel* and especially *Batman v Superman: Dawn of Justice*. Each viewing also uncovers another layer or meaning.

After all, Snyder is "the king of easter eggs, tossing so many of them into each of his movies that people are still finding them today."[161] The clear homages and lifting from the source material in his films are clear from the beginning. There are large lifts from *The Dark Knight Returns* and *The Death of Superman* to smaller nods like Lex Luthor's prison number designation tying into his first appearance in Action Comics, the Pb lead markings on Batman's Kryptonite grenades, the phone line referring to the year and issue of *The Death of Superman* comic, and Diana rolling her eyes at Lex's incorrect retelling of history.

Then there is the brilliant "Knightmare" sequence that was baffling to many casual viewers, but was packed with hints including Flash using a Time Boom, a Joker card taped to the gun and (possible) foreshadowing of the future, including Superman being susceptible to the Anti-Life Equation and Batman standing on the ruins of the Hall of Justice.

The difficulty in laying bread crumbs in one film to be picked up in another is that the opportunity to make those future films may never come. Zack Snyder spent nearly a decade plotting this universe full of weaving, interconnected storylines and the

---

[161] "Why Zack Snyder Is the Best Comic Book Movie Director In the Business," *TheFilteCast* (September 7, 2016) http://www.theflitecast.com/posts/2016/9/7/why-zack-snyder-is-the-best-comic-book-movie-director-in-the-business.

realization of that sort of planning and vision requires time and patience:

"One thing is certain, the filmmaker had a vision and knew what he was doing by mining different story elements from the comics and weaving them into a cohesive film narrative — exactly how a shared cinematic universe should be done. Sure, the payoff might've still been a long way off, but at least he had a clear creative direction."[162]

Recently, Snyder has been using the social media site Vero to share behind-the-scenes photos, answer fan questions, and explain some of the layers in the films and there is much more than just easter eggs and references[163] to the comics and future films to be found. It is clear to everyone that these films were meticulously planned, with seemingly innocuous (or confounding) scenes or throwaway lines actually playing larger roles, either symbolically or as a setup for future stories. And his fans cannot get enough:

"Sndyer's time in the DCEU may now be done, but that doesn't mean the analysis of his work in this universe is. He's developed a very passionate fanbase over the years, something that is always on display when it comes to discussing *Man of Steel*, *BvS*, or even Snyder's original plans for *Justice League Part 1 & 2*."[164]

Man of Steel presents Superman as a metaphor for Christ — with Zod acting as the Antichrist — from the miraculous way he was conceived, to his being sent here from the sky by his father to help the people of Earth — Jor-El even says to him, "You can save

---

[162] Dumaraog, Ana, "Zack Snyder Reveals Why Superman Is Evil in BvS' Knightmare Scene," *ScreenRant* (April 1, 2018) https://screenrant.com/zack-snyder-evil-superman-bvs-knightmare/.

[163] Cecchini, Mike. "Batman v Superman: Dawn of Justice – Complete DC Comics Easter Eggs and Reference Guide," *DenOfGeek* (March 25, 2019) https://www.denofgeek.com/comics/batman-v-superman-dawn-of-justice-complete-dc-comics-easter-eggs-and-reference-guide/.

[164] Hood, Cooper, "Zack Snyder Confirms BvS Flash Is from the Knightmare Timeline," *ScreenRant* (April 6, 2018) https://screenrant.com/zack-snyder-batman-v-superman-flash-knightmare-timeline/

all of them"— to struggling with his powers and the responsibility they place upon him like Jesus in the Garden of Gethsemane before ultimately accepting his fate at the age of 33.

It also examined the relationship between Objectivism and Christianity[165] in our current culture. The Christian allegory and biblical references do not end in *Man of Steel*, but are even more abundant in *Batman v Superman*, a film so full of meanings and symbolism that it led to a fan-led, Snyder-endorsed #BvSReferences challenge contest to find as many meanings as possible, such as the juxtaposition of Superman reaching out from skulls in the *Man of Steel* death vision and the people in skeleton face paintings reaching for him after he saves a girl during a Día de los Muertos celebration.

Zod represents the Antichrist and Lex Luthor is the representation of Satan, specifically from *Paradise Lost*.[166] Thus, if Superman is Jesus, then he must sacrifice himself to save the world.

"Earlier in the film, Lex [Luthor] complained that 'no man in the sky' intervened to save him from 'daddy's fists and abominations,' yet when Doomsday awakens, his first act is to punch Luthor and Superman stops him. Why save the man that is trying to destroy you? Christianity teaches that Jesus loves everyone, including sinners and even Judas, the man that betrayed him — 'forgive them, for they know not what they do.'"[167]

There is much more than just Clark as Christ.

There are the biblical allusions of horses signifying death —

---

[165] Bowyer, Charles, "The Metaphysics of Batman v Superman: A 15,000 Word Analysis," *ComicBookDebate* (November 23, 2017)
https://comicbookdebate.com/2017/11/23/the-metaphysics-of-batman-v-superman/.

[166] "BvS Reference: Lex Luthor Is the Allegorical Satan from Paradise Lost," *CinemaCure* (April 10, 2018)
https://cinemacure.wordpress.com/2018/04/10/bvs-reference-lex-luthor-is-the-allegorical-satan-from-paradise-lost/.

[167] u/lensgana, "Discussion: Superman Saving Lex from Doomsday's Fist in BvS," Reddit (August 13, 2017)
https://www.reddit.com/r/DC_Cinematic/comments/6thzag/discussion_superman_saving_lex_from_doomsdays/.

perhaps even referencing the four horsemen of the apocalypse (or Apokolips). There is Batman believing the "lie of the light" and, as a result, the omnipresent darkness of the film representing the feelings of the characters and the rain eventually acting as a baptism. Even the controversial "Martha" scene is full of character insights and meaningful layers for anyone that took a moment to realize them (like the accurate reaction of a triggered PTSD patient).[168]

There are references to other works, as well, ranging from John Boorman's 1981 film *Excalibur* (Superman and Batman are akin to King Arthur and Lancelot) to Greek mythology — when Luthor is staring at Zod's body in the genesis chamber, he invokes Icarus, telling Zod he "flew too close to the Sun," which Snyder confirmed holds a double meaning as too close to the Son of Krypton.[169]

There are also clear allusions to 9/11, the resulting xenophobia, and the media's role in shaping how we interact with our current society.

This also plays into the psychology of the characters themselves and informs their actions:

> "The main theme of the movie is how we project things that aren't necessarily true onto others. Batman projects all his fears and feelings of powerlessness onto Superman, Lex all his issues with God and his father. Superman likewise projects all his fears and insecurities onto Batman. Don't forget one of the most important lines in the movie, 'We've always created icons in our image and projected things onto them. Maybe he's not this devil or Christ

---

[168] Ng, Cherry, "The Controversial 'Martha' Leitmotif in Batman v Superman: Dawn of Justice," *Medium* (April 6, 2016)
https://medium.com/@cherrynghh/the-controversial-martha-leitmotif-in-batman-v-superman-dawn-of-justice-58f02c5035c4.

[169] Cavanaugh, Patrick, "Batman v Superman: Zack Snyder Confirms Icarus Double Meaning," *ComicBook* (March 30, 2018)
https://comicbook.com/dc/news/batman-v-superman-dawn-of-justice-zack-snyder-icarus-krypton/.

character, maybe he's just a guy trying to do the right thing.' I think this describes Superman exactly in the movie. They go out of their way in the film to show you how human and imperfect Kal is, more than almost any other version of the character. Then they contrast and contradict this with very blatant Christ symbolism. I think this was Snyder's way of involving the audience and showing us that we project things just as much as the characters in the movie. We are shown time and time again that Superman is just as messed up and human as the rest of us, but the overt symbolism and parallels makes us project this idea onto him when it's clearly not true. It was Lex who sees Superman as a Christ analog and its made very clear he's psychotic, so I don't think that's the message the movie wants us to take away."[170]

That is only scratching the surface. There are literally hundreds more, of which Snyder and screenwriter Chris Terrio chose their ten favorite fan entries.

There is a cadre of individuals that believe the since Snyder is explaining all of these details, it "proves it's not a good film."[171] After all, if you have to explain it, then you failed as a filmmaker, right? But he's only explaining them because (a) there are others that found these references and asked him about them and (b) furthermore, he wasn't given the chance to pay it all off in future films. If there is no ending, it's only natural for people to wonder what that ending would have been.

The dictum in directing a film is "show, don't tell." And he did that. Yet critics were confused, so he then told, and they in turn criticized him for having to tell them. How is one supposed to escape that circular logic?

---

[170] u/t0rche, "Death of Superman Concept Art / Jesus Lifted Down from Cross," Reddit (May 11, 2016)
https://www.reddit.com/r/DC_Cinematic/comments/4iygfb/death_of_superman_concept_art_jesus_lifted_down/.

[171] Arvedon, Jon, "Snyder's Need to Explain BvS Again & Again Proves It's Not a Good Film," *CBR* (April 5, 2018)
https://www.cbr.com/zack-snyder-explaining-batman-v-superman/.

Zack Snyder never talks down to his audience, but it's clear that his detractors insist that he should employ the most basic, lowest common denominator storytelling and dismiss anything more: "These truly are academic allusions, symbols, and imagery being discussed in the context of how they shape the film as a piece of art...and easter eggs are not the same thing. Movie reviews outlining the reasons a film is 'the worse [sic] ever' are not the same thing. And critics using their position to make conversation and the sharing of different opinions *more difficult* are not the same thing."[172]

Few, if any, superhero films have been studied and analyzed the way *Man of Steel* and *Batman v Superman* have been — and continue to be — and that's something that cannot be captured by a Rotten Tomatoes score.

VII. A Heroic Cast

While his films are still pored over and scrutinized, it certainly seems that Snyder's most enduring legacy at DC will be his casting. In the midst of all of the criticisms and questions regarding the films, no one questioned the actors he chose. Even his harshest critics can agree with that: "No matter what you think of his film-making style, Snyder's casting of the DCEU's principal characters is an area where he's consistently hit the nail on the head."[173]

His colleagues agree.

Wonder Woman director Patty Jenkins called the choice of

---

[172] Dyce, Andrew, "Batman v Superman Fans Have Shown Where 'Critics' Failed," *ScreenRant* (April 24, 2018)
https://screenrant.com/batman-v-superman-critics-failed-snyder-fans/.
[173] Matadeen, Renaldo, "Zack Snyder's Greatest DCEU Legacy Is Casting," *CBR* (June 30, 2017)
https://www.cbr.com/zack-snyder-dceu-casting/.

Gal Gadot a "magical gift"[174] and admitted that Snyder and his crew did a better job of casting than she would have done while *Aquaman* director James Wan called Snyder's casting of Jason Momoa "a stroke of genius."[175] Gadot, Momoa, and Fisher were diverse choices and give the DCEU a more universal feel — white Americans aren't the only ones that can be superheroes.

The direction — and directors — of the DC film universe may be changing, but the majority of actors are not. Fans and critics alike love the casting choices Snyder made — and his casts love him. They defended him against the whirlwind of negative reviews of the first two films and bought into his vision.[176]

When Ray Fisher displayed his "I Love ZS" t-shirt at Comic-Con, it was initially received as a sort of sympathy card for Snyder after the tragic passing of his daughter. However, as news of the drama and mismanagement behind *Justice League* began to emerge and word spread that Snyder had actually been fired, the statement took on a different meaning. Fisher, who like the rest of the cast was presumably contractually prevented from speaking honestly on the matter, was still making his feelings known.

Much of the universe's cinematic future is full of doubts and confusion and there is certainly work to be done, but finding the right actors to portray DC's mightiest heroes isn't an issue.

It's already been handled beautifully.

---

[174] Schwerdtfeger, Conner, "Why Patty Jenkins Wouldn't Have Cast Gal Gadot as Wonder Woman," *CinemaBlend* (June 9, 2017)
https://www.cinemablend.com/news/1668549/why-patty-jenkins-wouldnt-have-cast-gal-gadot-as-wonder-woman

[175] Verhoeven, Beatrice, "How Aquaman Director James Wan Will Wash the Silliness from Oceanic Hero," TheWrap (August 10, 2017)
https://www.thewrap.com/james-wan-removing-aquaman-stigma-silliness-jason-momoa/.

[176] Begley, Chris, "Amy Adams Talks Justice League Morale, Praises Zack Snyder after Batman v Superman Backlash," *Batman-News* (September 12, 2016)
https://batman-news.com/2016/09/12/amy-adams-justice-league-morale-zack-snyder/.

VIII. The Future

So what comes next?

While there have been more DC releases that were more traditional and, as a result, better reviewed, Snyder's shadow still looms large over Metropolis, Gotham, Themyscira, and everywhere in between. Even if he is no longer there, his "vision for the DC remains in the DNA of its heroes."[177]

Ingrained audience expectations, gleefully malevolent reviews, and a panicky movie studio desperate to shortcut the process in an attempt to catch its rival all led to the premature departure of a filmmaker that had grand plans, took risks, packed his films full of references and symbolism, and clearly loved these characters and the books from which their stories came. Snyder brought a graphic novel to life on the big screen and he delivered superhero films that were unlike anything ever seen before — and possibly ever again.

Realizing the groundwork he laid and the plans he had for future films, it's almost depressing to think about what could have been. Sure, we're finally getting the Snyder Cut of Justice League, but it's not the same as it could have been.

The Zack Snyder era is over and "the DC Movie Universe is worse off because of it."[178]

---

[177] Dyce, Andrew, "The DC Movie Universe Is Worse Without Zack Snyder," *ScreenRant* (November 27, 2017) https://screenrant.com/zack-snyder-dceu-movie-universe-future/2/.
[178] Dyce, Andrew, "The DC Movie Universe Is Worse Without Zack Snyder," *ScreenRant* (November 27, 2017) https://screenrant.com/zack-snyder-dceu-movie-universe-future/2/.

Why Ava DuVernay's *When They See Us* Is The Torturous Masterclass In Systemic Assault
by Ezinne Ukoha[179]

When they say boys, they're not talking about us.
When did we get to be boys?

As the daughter of Nigerian parents who followed the mass exodus of the early seventies from a war-torn country, thanks to the failure of Biafra and the remnants of an uncertain future, my eventual conception and birth in the United States of America was considered the ultimate blessing.

The family of four that included the addition of a younger brother, departed the temperate Midwest for the systemized chaos of the unregulated wilderness of a former colonial territory, that was ablaze with the normalized disease of bribery and corruption, that filled the path to much-needed progression with potholes of nationalized dysfunction.

As civil servants, my parents had bought the falsehood of how returning to your homeland with foreign degrees would somehow make the trajectory of enjoying the fruits of your labor seamlessly attainable.

Unfortunately the only way to survive the gangster era of bloody military coups, scarcity of homegrown resources and ac-

---

[179] Ezinne Ukoha is an essayist, poet and burgeoning screenwriter, who maintains a blog on Medium where she tackles the subjects of racial inequality, politics and pop culture. She obtained a Bachelor of Arts in English from the University of Missouri, Kansas City, and has since written for HuffPost, Essence magazine and MadameNoire to name a few. She also worked as a web producer for Tastemade, ABC Digital and MSN. She is currently working on a book of short stories.

cessibility to basic amenities, was to convert into a tribal hoodlum, with the motivation to do whatever it takes to sustain a functional household.

My childhood was decent, although the shock of being uprooted from the comfortable existence of Kansas City to the heated metropolis of Lagos, did pose a myriad of challenges that only worsened once I entered boarding school at the age of eleven.

But as we all know, it takes the tousle with grittiness to build a tough exterior, and so while my parents weathered the terrain of navigating career goals without stepping on the booby traps of standardized gluttony — I was also tasked with the assignment of keeping my head above water under the care of cruel housemistresses — while counting down the days to my heavenly departure for the birth country that was waiting to rescue me.

The first thing that struck me when I cautiously submitted myself to the poignant four-part Netflix series *When They See Us*, which was spectacularly written, produced, and directed by the national treasure known as Ava DuVernay — was the glaring fact that those boys were around my age at the time of their unfortunate encounter with the jaws of a bigoted machine.

Another jarring realization that hovered was the juxtaposition in the circumstances that cradled our destinies.

Towards the end of 1989, I was a sixteen-years-old student who was trying to get through her A-levels in anticipation for the triumphant return to America to begin a new life on a college campus, that would yield the promise of better tomorrows without the buzzkill of a stiflingly warped society.

Antron McCray, Kevin Richardson, Yusef Salaam, Raymond Santana and Korey Wise were teenage boys (NOT MEN), based in the city of my dreams, New York, who were entrapped in a furious war, that featured a treacherous battlefield, with the poisoned shrapnel that was aimed at the formulated pungency of darkened hues.

It was an indescribable rattling effect that overcame my senses as I endured the irony of how elated I was to escape the crippling disposition of my homeland for the embrace of my civilized and tolerant birthplace, just as five American boys of color were being brutally persecuted by a toxic judicial system, that continues to follow those deadly blueprints without skipping a beat.

Africans in America during the sixties and seventies were righteously misled by White supremacists, who pretended to care under the guise of stealing ownership of a narrative that they recklessly distorted with multitude of lies about how American-born Blacks were the scum of the earth with lazy tendencies, and acute envy for African Blacks, who were able to successfully assimilate in the country that graciously nurtured their ambitious pursuits.

But thankfully, young adulthood permitted the the architecture of my own personalized views based on experience and observation.

And the summation of my thoughts as an American-born Nigerian definitely makes *When They See Us* particularly torturous to internalize when you consider the early years of heightened anticipation, that was boosted by the encouragement of my naive parents, who are now well-aware of how the country they idolized betrayed them through the tinted lenses of disingenuousness.

America was never beautiful. America was never blessed by God. America was never built on the foundation of equality. America never extended the duty of humanness to non-Whites.

Slavery Never Ended

Ava DuVernay has created a canvass of love for Black and Brown eyes that hurt as much as it validates the awfulness of never-ending pain, that stings the eyes and pierces the heart with stark imagery of the outright violation of our bodies in formation.

Yes, it was hard to watch the tearful pleas and desperation from helpless parents, who were forced to witness the pulverizing process of the Black and Brown bodies that they made with the hope that they would flourish without incidence.

Yes, it was hard to watch these Black and Brown children being categorized as adult villains in a scheming pact that featured White men and White women scrounging around like a pack of wolves with deadened eyes and salivating demeanors gathered for the slaughter.

But the hardest part was recalling how eager I was as a youngster to claim a country that I thought was pure and fair, when it was and still is the basin of hell for those who resemble my template.

I could've easily been the sister or cousin of one of the Black teenage boys. A regular lad with an adventurous spirit, and all the makings of a future success, with the great misfortune of fitting the slot that mandates entry into the criminalized cells of a biased society.

The brutal truth is that I could still be the sister of a Black man who tries to reach for his wallet, and gets hit multiple times by bullets from the gun of a rogue White cop. And I might have to deal with a gang of White men with badges, beating me down so hard that I can barely keep my frock on my battered and bruised Black body, while White patrons capture, upload and share for the highest bidder.

Ava DuVernay's masterpiece is surely a masterclass in the systemic assault of Black and Brown bodies. And that thorough education that graphically details the demonization of Black children by the cowardly product of Whiteness, has been diligently prepared for the palettes of clueless White folks, who annoyingly challenge the endorsement of their privilege on a daily basis.

One of the lines from the dramatic series that hit hard was when one of the boys who was released as a scarred man, asked:

When they say boys, they're not talking about us. When did we get to be boys?

And that's the crux of the nightmare that gripped the innocent lives of these poor young souls, who were swiftly enslaved by the supremacy of Whiteness, that dictates the urgency of stealing away the youthful zeal that White teens are able to rambunctiously indulge in with little or no interference from those who cosign that level of freedom until darker hues come into focus.

Exactly thirty years later, and the practice of vilifying Black youths with threats and fatal bullet wounds is still the standard default for law enforcement.

Not too long ago, a twitter account belonging to the Baltimore Police[180], unleashed a severe warning to officers in the downtown area, who were responding to an active situation that might have mimicked that night in 1989, when Black youths congregated at Central Park, and a handful were plucked for systemic extinction.

In 2019, a high-ranking officer can tweet out his extreme tendencies for the world to see, under the tutelage of a bigoted president, who once waged a highly-visible campaign[181] to have five Black and Brown teenage boys slaughtered for a crime he knew they didn't commit.

Sgt. Mike Mancuso can lawfully order his officers to treat Black kids like hardened criminals if need be — which is code for "kill first, and keep it moving."

What America exacted on the primed fragility of Antron McCray, Kevin Richardson, Yusef Salaam, Raymond Santana and

---

[180] Ukhoa, Ezinne, "Dear Baltimore Police, Please Stop Endorsing Systemic Brutality Against Black Youths", *Medium* (May 28, 2019)
https://medium.com/@nilegirl/dear-baltimore-police-please-stop-endorsing-systemic-brutality-against-black-youths-8eb9305f1373.
[181] Ryan, Patrick, "Ava DuVernay lets Trump 'speak for himself' in Central Park Five series 'When They See Us'," *USA Today* (June 3, 2019)
https://www.usatoday.com/story/life/tv/2019/06/03/looking-back-trumps-involvement-1989-central-park-five-case/1212335001/.

Korey Wise is not only gross miscarriage of justice, but it represents the undiluted verses of America's hidden National Anthem with the supremeness of the original American Horror Story.

This Is Why We Kneel

This is why the ugliness of a currently terminal nation can be botched by a self-professed White nationalist, who refuses to acknowledge the role he played in the quest to suffocate the lives of five American teenagers, who were easily expendable in his eyes

This is why the horrid White police officers and embattled persecutor Linda Fairstein[182] are able to sleep very well at night, despite the undisputed facts that prove how so very wrong they were, and why the potency of Whiteness can effortlessly handle the burden of guilt with the banner of how Blackness is evil enough to take the lifelong suffering that's deemed appropriate by calculating beasts of a mercilessly flawed system.

The America that I envisioned when I was young and impressionable enough to be dangerously influenced, has been revised to accommodate the bleaker and dire translation that terrorizes the consciousness, but empowers the gratified restoration of reality.

The gruesome assault of Black and Brown children is the unforgivable sin that this country will never atone for because of the blasphemous elements that even God in his omnipotency won't be able to wash away with the floods of cleansing.

This Isn't Just A "Black Thing"

White mothers and fathers can gawk with distanced fascination at the horrors of Black parenthood, but best believe that

---

[182] Grove, Lloyd, "Central Park Five Prosecutor Takes Fire Over Ava DuVernay Netflix Series, Calls It 'Basket of Lies'" *The Daily Beast* (June 4, 2019)
https://www.thedailybeast.com/when-they-see-us-central-park-five-prosecutor-takes-fire-over-ava-duvernay-netflix-series.

this blotted legacy of callousness that assaults our wombs and imprisons our young, is yours to claim, thanks to your pandering of Black pain and blissful inaction.

When you watch the skillful delivery of *When They See Us*, please pay attention to the expert commandeering of stellar cast members, and the way they instinctively respond to the bites of sorrow that consume their performances.

You have to see what they see, and when you do — there's no turning back.

In the realm of Black and Brown, we can't ever un-see it, but Whiteness will conveniently scrub away their stains with the limbs of our children.

Justice will never be served until we wipe away the supremacy in our midst using the same tactics of our oppressors that demands superiority at all costs.

The anger is good. The healing is power. Hunger for revenge is healthy.

Gratitude for visionaries is the currency for the security of our narratives that are packaged by us and for us.

Thank you, Ava.

"Stay away from the door!": The Women of John Carpenter's *The Fog*

by Sydney Urbanek[183]

"If there's one thing I've learned, it's that if there's a knock at the door, and it's at night, you don't open the door," says producer Debra Hill[184] in the DVD commentary for *The Fog* (1980), a film she also co-wrote.

It might sound like common sense to you the way it does to me, but the John Carpenter classic has some fun with the idea that it doesn't necessarily for everyone.

The Fog was Carpenter's first film after *Halloween*, the box-office smash that established Jamie Lee Curtis as a scream queen and redefined slasher movies forever. The former's plot takes place over a single day—April 21st, 1980—from midnight to midnight. It's the 100th birthday of Antonio Bay, a fictional coastal town in California, and its inhabitants are preparing for a candlelight procession to celebrate the milestone.

It's common knowledge that Antonio Bay was founded on the heels of a tragedy. On a particularly foggy night in 1880, a clipper ship called the *Elizabeth Dane* crashed into a rocky shore and sunk, leaving no survivors. But the community's dark secret is that the ship was lured to its fate by a campfire that had been placed there by six conspirators—the town's founding fathers. The

---

[183] Sydney Urbanek is a Toronto-based culture writer who recently finished a Cinema Studies MA program. She writes a newsletter called "Monoym Mythology" about mostly pop divas and their (visual) antics.

[184] Carr, Kevin, "19 Things We Learned from 'The Fog' Commentary," Film School Rejects (October 31, 2013) https://filmschoolrejects.com/19-things-we-learned-from-the-fog-commentary-ef8bde4fbeb1/.

Elizabeth Dane carried multiple people with leprosy who intended to start a colony "only a mile distant," under the leadership of a wealthy man named Blake. Wishing to eradicate the disease (and diseased people) on board, the conspirators orchestrated the ship's demise and then plundered it, using Blake's gold to build the town. Now, a century later, he and his ghost gang are back—and travelling via a thick, glowing fog—to kill six descendants of Antonio Bay's founding fathers.

The Fog's premise reads something like a Boy Scout ghost story come to life. (It actually begins with a town elder, Mr. Machen (John Houseman), sharing Antonio Bay's fabled curse[185] with a group of boys around a campfire.) Seafaring, which characterizes the town's current existence as much as its origin story, is also a stereotypically male domain. One gets the sense moving through the town that any woman who lives here is probably the child or spouse of a mariner, or perhaps the mother of one-to-be.

But despite the film's on-paper boyishness, Carpenter and Hill chose to structure the story largely around four women—all intelligent and resourceful, all terrorized by Blake and his fellow ghosts from their separate spheres. It's an understatement to say that *The Fog* is carried by radio host Stevie (Adrienne Barbeau), hitchhiker Elizabeth (Jamie Lee Curtis), civic leader Kathy (Janet Leigh), and Kathy's assistant, Sandy (Nancy Kyes). And, importantly, when 'there's a knock at the door, and it's at night,' none of these four women open it.

The men they share screen time with, on the other hand, are almost all either bland or thickheaded—the latter trait being responsible for more than one death in the film (read: they're prone to opening doors that they shouldn't). It's unclear how intentional all of this was, but the resulting story nevertheless becomes one about a

---

[185] Lounge, Chaz, "Opening to "The Fog," YouTube (October 31, 2006) https://www.youtube.com/watch?v=cwSbRKd_J8k&t=19s.

group of clever women cleaning up, and paying for, the misdeeds of six men who lived and died long ago.

At the film's centre is Stevie Wayne, the owner and host of KAB Radio, not to mention the lighthouse out of which the station operates. Stevie's a single mother—she has one son, Andy—who recently moved to Antonio Bay from Chicago. There's a father figure in the family photos she keeps at her bedside, but the weatherman, Dan, is established as her love interest in the film (albeit one she keeps at a distance), so we might assume that she's a widow.

Stevie's show has made her a local celebrity of sorts. On the air, she speaks slowly and deeply, her broadcast chock-full of sexual suggestiveness. Take, for instance, the following proposal: "Keep me turned on for a while, and I'll try my best to do the same for you." Her listener base is comprised of the mariners and other graveyard shifters of Antonio Bay; they tune in from the early evening until one o'clock in the morning—the end of what she calls the "witching hour." Seductive and a tad motherly, her voice is a welcome substitute for female company during their quiet and lonely evenings. When the film begins, it's audible in the hull of the ill-fated Seagrass, the men on board bonding over their shared crushes on Stevie. "Boy, would I like to meet her," says one. "I saw her at a grocery store one day," replies another.

But interestingly, Stevie doesn't actually appear on screen until 15 minutes into Carpenter's film; until then, we know her solely as a voice. One might argue that this is evidence of her objectification or disembodiment, but it's equally worth considering how her voice reaches and commands different spaces—to the point that she has perhaps the most agency of any of *The Fog*'s characters.

When Stevie picks up the phone to get the weather update from Dan, we realize that the voice she uses on the air is mostly affectation—something she can switch on and off. She's used it to build a dedicated audience of night owls but can stow it away during the day for grocery shopping and Little League games. Owing to the popularity of her station, it's also everywhere: Alongside her jazz and classical music selections[186], it's transmitted into many of Antonio Bay's homes, ships, cars, and workplaces. By default, this means that a great deal of *The Fog*'s music is diegetic (with everything else being Carpenter's official score for the film[187]). Stevie therefore controls much of *The Fog*'s soundscape, even when saying nothing at all. She may seem isolated from the rest of the film's characters, but her show actually connects her to them in personal, even intimate ways. After all, she DJs Elizabeth and Nick's first night together, which also happens to be the men of the *Seagrass*'s last.

The ubiquity of Stevie's voice and her view from the lighthouse both work together to make her the eyes of Antonio Bay. Once Blake and his ghosts begin their revenge spree, she gives the other characters live updates regarding the fog's position in the town. Over the phone, she frantically begs Dan[188] not to open the door for the fog when it (very politely) knocks, but, high on his own arrogance, he does. After the ghosts have slaughtered him and disconnected the town's phone lines, Stevie takes to her broadcast to have Elizabeth and Nick rescue Andy from her home. She then has the characters congregate in the town's old church, saving most of their lives in the process. And, crucially, when the fog comes knocking at her own door, she not only doesn't open it but attempts to block it with a ladder.

While Stevie's voice is the only thing connecting her to the *Seagrass* — the ship carrying *The Fog*'s first victims[189] — the other

---

[186] GSS, Society, Soundtrack, Greek, "KAB Radio, Antonio Bay - The Complete Source Tracks (John Carpenter's The Fog - 1980)," YouTube (November 9, 2016) https://www.youtube.com/watch?v=KegXHq9VNFI.
[187] Lewallen, Clint, "the fog expanded soundtrack by john carpenter," YouTube (December 27, 2012) https://www.youtube.com/watch?v=zKGzUxH9GyQ.
[188] Factory, Shout!, "Meathook to the Throat! (2/3) The Fog (1980)," YouTube (July 31, 2013) https://www.youtube.com/watch?v=kf-UHx45R2I.
[189] Factory, Shout!, "The Fog Murders its First Victims! (3/3) The Fog (1980)," YouTube (July 31, 2013) https://www.youtube.com/watch?v=cam-PPPC9h8.

three women are linked to it directly through their relationships. Kathy Williams hasn't heard from her husband since he went out with the rest of the ship's crew last night, but she's mostly preoccupied with Antonio Bay's 100th birthday celebrations as the town's civic leader. Kathy's a high-strung, no-bullshit public figure who's joined at the hip by her deadpan assistant, Sandy. The two women couldn't be more different, and that's precisely why they vibe so well. "You can be a very annoying person at times, but you do keep me together," Kathy tells Sandy, lovingly. "Thank you, Mrs. Williams," Sandy responds, recalling the monotone of *The Graduate*'s Ben.

When the two women visit Father Malone (Hal Holbrook) to confirm that he'll give the blessing at the procession that night, they find the front door already open. It's the only one that either of them is faced with during the film—it's also daytime and no ghosts have knocked on it, to be clear—but they nevertheless react the way one ought to upon discovering something ominous. "Not a good sign," Sandy says, sounding almost bored. Kathy and Sandy are unfortunately *The Fog*'s only women to interact with one another before the entire cast congregates at the church, but their collegial friendship and the fact that they seem to have been written as a package deal make them seemingly less vulnerable to its threat.

More tangibly impacted by the ghosts is Nick (Tom Atkins), a fisherman and close friend of the men aboard the *Seagrass*. He quickly involves the coast guard when the crew doesn't come home, but he also picks up Elizabeth—a hitchhiker-turned-fling—over the course of the night. As a result, her storyline is collapsed into his, and what she expects to be a fun overnighter turns into something much more dire.

Elizabeth is quickly established as a freewheeler. When she tells Nick that he's her 13th ride and he jokes that he's unlucky, she teases, "We'll see." They sleep together within the hour, only exchanging names afterwards, and Elizabeth reveals that she was raised wealthy but is, by choice, hitchhiking her way to Vancouver to try and make it as an artist. And, just then, there's a knock at his door. Elizabeth stays put, pulling the sheets slightly closer to her body, but Nick instantly hops out of bed to answer it. He's saved only by the fact that the clock strikes one in the morning, the time that the six conspirators finished devising their cruel plan a hundred years prior. The ghosts have dissipated by the time Nick gets the door open, but the point is that he still opens the door.

It's notable that in most of the scenes shared by Elizabeth and Nick, she bears the brunt of the ghosts' terrorism, despite not even being a resident of Antonio Bay. In what is perhaps her most famous scene in the film, a ghost possesses the corpse of Dick Baxter, one of the men killed on the *Seagrass*, and approaches her with a scalpel in the coroner's office. She later becomes a sort of surrogate mother to Andy when Stevie can't physically be there to save him. As ThoughtPusher wrote for Bitch Flicks[190] in 2016, "The woman who fills the carefree Hitcher role is embroiled in the strange happenings of the cursed town and answers the call to save a child in need."

Ultimately, the only woman in the film who *does* open the door for the fog is Mrs. Kobritz (Regina Waldon), Andy's babysitter. She dies instantly[191], but in fairness to her, there's no knock. Plus, the scene in question isn't characterized by the same sort of hubris as Dan's death scene. Mrs. Kobritz is visibly frightened, and ensures that Andy is in his room before venturing out into the fog. She inadvertently saves his life as a result, and so her death doubles as a sort of sacrifice made on his behalf.

---

[190] ThoughtPusher, "'The Fog': 5 Women, an Environmental Crisis, and No Forecast of Friendship," *Bitch Flicks* (July 2, 2016)
http://www.btchflcks.com/2016/07/the-fog-5-women-an-environmental-crisis-and-no-forecast-of-friendship.html#.X4XgZ3hKg-c.
[191] Factory, Shout!, "The Fog Kills Grandma (1/3) The Fog (1980)," YouTube (July 31, 2013) https://www.youtube.com/watch?v=5SmLFd6ZldY.

And that's the thing: the women of this film go extraordinary lengths to save the men of Antonio Bay, or to keep them company while they run for their lives. No one expects Mrs. Kobritz to die for Andy, or Stevie to guide the other characters to safety, or Kathy to put on a smile for the town while her husband's missing, or Elizabeth to stay in this ghastly town with Nick. But without these women and their actions, *The Fog* would be a 10-minute short of men gladly opening doors for ghosts.

'We Are Too Rare':
The Importance of Inclusivity Behind Spike Lee's *She's Gotta Have It* Reboot

by Katie Tandy[192]

"For the first time, I was with people of color occupying both sides of the screen, stamping our perspectives on history."

In 1985, a young man by the name of Spike Lee had the audacity to write, direct, produce, and star in a film about female sexuality. The plot revolved around a young black woman — Nola Darling — who, Lee described[193], is "living her life like a man," a woman deftly toggling between three lovers, unabashedly voracious for sex.

I speak of course of *She's Gotta Have It*, the black and white, Brooklyn-set film made for $175,000 that pulled in $7 million. As *The New York Times* wrote in 1987, "For an independent, shoestring production, this was remarkable. For an independent shoestring production by a black man about black people, it was astounding."

The film's candor, humor, and unrelenting examination of gender, race, class, and sexuality rocketed Lee not just into the arts scene, but placed him at the nexus of black culture.

Lee has gone on to direct 76 film projects—from documen-

---

[192] Katie Tandy is a memoirist, playwright, and co-founding editor of PULP, an online arts and culture publication centering sex/uality, reproductive rights, and all things body. She is working on a forthcoming memoir braiding stories from her childhood with human physiology. When she's not writing, she's singing with the Oakland rock band The Shattucks.
[193] Mieher, Stuart, "Spike Lee's She's Gotta Have It," The New York Times (August 9, 1987) https://www.nytimes.com/1987/08/09/magazine/spike-lee-s-gotta-have-it.html.

taries and video shorts, to feature length films including *Do The Right Thing*, *Jungle Fever*, *Malcolm X*, *Chi-Raq*, and *Rodney King*. Throughout his career, he's tasked himself with taking aim at some of the most complicated sociocultural dialogues on the goddamn planet.

The kind of pressure related to such work is, of course, largely untenable. How does one remain the proverbial provocateur, the voice of a generation, of a race?

One answer would be to return to your roots, to the very thing that begot the vision that put you on the map. And so, 30 years later, we find ourselves on Netflix, poised for the revamp of *She's Gotta Have It*, a 10-part series that will plunge us back into Brooklyn, back into Nola's bedroom, to see just how far we've come.

Or … to see just how much we've stagnated.

Ironically, if we'd all evolved as much as we would have liked in the past three decades, *She's Gotta Have It* would be terribly passé.

But alas, it perhaps feels more poignant than ever. And in no small part due to the fact that Lee, a man, is writing Nola's story *again*—a story predicated on what many now call "Black Girl Magic"— surfacing complicated criticisms that have haunted the film since its inception. bell hooks took aim at *She's Gotta Have It* in her scathing essay[194] "Whose Pussy Is This?" which examines the infamously humiliating and brutal rape scene of Nola in the original film.

> *"Overall it is the men who speak in 'She's Gotta Have It.' While Nola appears one-dimensional in perspective and focus, seemingly more concerned about her sexual relationships than about any other aspect of her life, the male characters are multidimensional. They have personalities. Nola has no personality…Her one claim to fame is that she likes to fuck. In the male pornographic imagination she could be*

---

[194] Hooks, Bell, *Talking Back: Thinking Feminist, Thinking Black* (1989) https://books.google.com/books/about/Talking_Back.html?id=MpN0ikR6-f4C.

described as *"pure pussy,"* that is to say her ability to perform sexually is the central, defining aspect of her identity."

Disturbingly, in the wake of being raped, Nola—at first—insists upon her own celibacy, and then monogamy with her lover Jamie, the very man who raped her.

To his credit, Lee has spoken at length about how problematic this rape scene was, calling it his "biggest regret"[195] and promising, "there will be nothing like that in *She's Gotta Have It*, the TV show, that's for sure."

The film remains — like much art — confounding, fraught, and for many, in opposition to feminist ideals, despite also being visionary, progressive, and at least *intending* to advance the dialogue around gender equality.

Which is to say nothing of its undeniable power in placing black voices at the center of cultural commentary.

This is all to say, I wanted to talk to someone behind the project who had similar stakes to Nola — a Black, queer, sex-positive artist who was tasked in recreating Nola Darling, a compelling and provocative heroine for the 21st century.

The Establishment caught up with Janis Vogel, an assistant editor on *She's Gotta Have It*, who worked hand-in-hand with Lee to make this show one of the most hotly anticipated of the season.

Katie:

So much and so little has changed since 1986 — society is strange that way. But if these themes on race, power, sexuality, feminism and "success" weren't still potently relevant, the remake wouldn't be happening. What are you thoughts on how these themes have evolved between the original film and this series?

---

[195] Jr., Fleming, Mike, "No Cannes Do: Why Spike Lee Nixed 'Do The Right Thing' Silver Anniversary For Black Fest Fete," *Deadline* (May 13, 2014)
https://deadline.com/2014/05/no-cannes-do-why-spike-lee-nixed-do-the-right-thing-silver-anni-for-black-fest-fete-729355/.

Why is Nola's story still important?

Janis:

It's true, so many themes touched on in the original are still painfully relevant today, and whether it's narrative or documentary work, as many voices as possible need to be shedding light on the fact that the world has not improved enough for people of color, women, the LGBTQIA community, and so many others.

In *She's Gotta Have It*, Spike Lee has created and recreated a strong black female lead, played by the powerful DeWanda Wise. *She's Gotta Have It* was made in 1986 and is the story of a woman who is labeled a freak for having multiple lovers. He has started a conversation, which I have been a part of, a conversation that continuously needs to be challenged.

Spike is challenging viewpoints that, as in 1986, are still predominant oppressive areas of culture today (monogamy, sexuality, gender expression, career choice, fashion, rape culture, police violence). This narrative is still relevant thirty years later and means a lot to me personally. As part of the next generation of filmmakers I want to continue this conversation, and want to challenge all media to continue pushing the boundaries and shattering the narrow viewpoints that perpetuate a toxic environment. Spike wants to challenge the status quo, and continuously states that Nola is just one woman's story and there is room for many more.

I look forward to the discussions that arise when the show airs on November 25. I can't wait to experience the heated debates the show will inspire knowing that I was a part of making the world talk about black women, race, gender, slavery, Trump—and so much more, *everything* that must never be swept under the proverbial rug.

Katie:

It's no secret that film and television (as with almost every occupation on earth with the exception of nurses, teachers, and social workers) is dominated by white men. Having a queer woman of color like yourself work on the post production team for this story feels particularly poignant. What are your thoughts on how your personal identity intersects with the content of the series, as well as how it disrupts the demographics of this industry writ large?

Janis:

Women of color behind the camera—we are too rare. People trust what they're familiar with, and editing is a position of trust. Editors are trusted with the images of the film, entrusted with the task of making meaning of disparate frames of action and sound. The two editors on *She's Gotta Have It*, Hye Mee Na and Randy Wilkens were both people of color and were the ones who initially brought me onto the project. I in turn was able to have a hand in hiring two additional women onto our team, Jacqueline Basse and Briana Stodden. I have worked on shows where, I am the only woman or only woman of color in the room, so this was a rare opportunity to be in an environment where that norm was basically reversed.

At one particular screening I remember being very conscious of the fact that for the first time in my career, I was in a room with solely people of color occupying both sides of the screen. We were making films, making cultural currency, stamping our perspectives on history. I relished it all in a silent inner high five.

That experience was invaluable, necessary, for me as a person of color to not just know that was possible, but to live it. I was having conversations with my coworkers that I had never had on other jobs. Our water-cooler discussions were about race, gender, sexuality — which is not always the case in the film industry. It is our responsibility to normalize these conversations.

While I was working on the show, I was also co-president of an organization, The Blue Collar Post Collective. We advocate for more inclusiveness in the film industry and support emerging and transitioning talent in post production. When there were job openings on *She's Gotta Have It*, I was able to pull from our membership, and thereby embody our mission to make the industry more accessible. It's so important to pull other people up with us as we rise—to not see success as a competitive edge, but as an opportunity for those beside and below us to succeed as well.

In August 2017, scenes from SGHI premiered at the Martha's Vineyard African American Film Festival, which was held in my high school. Sponsored by HBO, the festival was in its 15th year. At the festival I watched an episode of *Insecure* with Spike and when I asked him if the show was "the competition" he reminded me that there is room for more than one black female narrative.

Nola does not represent all black women. There is so much room for everyone on both sides of the screen. Spike Lee is using his voice to talk about women of color, men of color, race, and politics in America. There is still a long way to go, a lot more voices to hear from.

Katie:

I think, to be honest, the biggest distraction for me in the movie were the three male lovers — they were all so infantile and exhausting in their own way. I never believed this brilliant, confident woman would be dealing with any of them. I obviously disagree with bell here, but to me, the men are broadly sketched, their nuances as people unexplored. Does the series better tackle these men as different-but-compelling entities to Nola as there is more screen-time to explore them and their myriad relationships?

Janis:

Spike asked me one day, "which team are you on?" as in which of Nola's lovers do I root for most.

It was *tempting* to say Mars, because Spike played Mars. I said Greer. "Greer?! Greer?!" he said. Spike was shocked. It became a recurring question he liked to ask people—Spike likes teams. He would regularly say to us "6:30am bat-time," and then later, "bat-time same time tomorrow." I think this team-orientedness is reflected in his storytelling. He seems to like clear differentiation between characters, while still rendering the characters more than caricatures; his characters end up breaking the molds of stereotype in unpredictable ways.

"It's so important to pull other people up with us as we rise."

Katie:

One of thee most chilling scenes in the movie to me is Nola's nightmare that three other black women want to burn her alive for stealing their men…for being a "whore," for tainting the few "good black men" around. It's a short but deeply painful and powerful scene that deals with the respectability politics of being black in America — especially as a young single woman of color who is sexually empowered. It's a brief schism in Nola's confidence that we get to bear witness to.

Janis:

Nola's confidence is definitely tested in the series. Nola demands respect even while she is exploring her options, not just in terms of lovers, but in terms of her whole self expression.

The female characters in this series question each other's choices. But rather than feeling like a shaming nightmare, the series tries to promote the idea that friends should check each other. They aren't resentment-free—one friend says, "we can't all be like Nola, dating three hot dudes at once." On the other hand, throughout the series Nola is faced with men shaming women and victim-blaming.

And Nola doesn't put up with objectification or judgment on any level. In this sense, she is a role model to all women. She refuses to be a victim, to hide. Nola wants it all: She wants to be revealing, she wants to sleep with multiple people, and she demands respect—anything less is a waste of her time.

This is not because she is impervious to pain or conflict. She goes to therapy; she is vulnerable; she faces challenges in her every-day life. In this sense, she is a role model to all women, not via invincibility, but via being human.

Katie:
I've never been called "sick" in response to the joy I derive from sex, but I've certainly had to explain (again and again) why it feels important to my own feminism to be really vocal and visible about my physical pleasure…can you talk a little bit about the celebration of female sexuality in the series?

Janis:
The series definitely opens up a conversation about female sexuality — her own sexuality is one of the major sectors of identity Nola is processing. While broadening her definitions, Nola defines her own boundaries and rules very strongly. She defines herself as a "sex-positive, polyamorous, pansexual" person; her therapist reacts with raised eyebrows.

I would say, more than celebrating sexual fluidity, the series plays the role of keeping that dialogue alive. Nola celebrates and defends her own freedom, faces consequences, and ultimately makes difficult choices surrounding her sexuality. She's navigating obstacles and complications that arise due to her sexuality—she is defining herself against the "norm" represented by the perspectives of her lovers, who themselves vary in their adherence to norms and morals of any standard sort. Still, the series seems to ask, can Nola have everything—even 30 years later?

Three decades later, from rude comments on the street, accusations by close friends and lovers (one calls her a sex-addict), to sexual assault—all the forms of repression explored in the film are included, and rightfully so, in the series.

Katie:
What can "happen" in a TV series that you can't achieve with a film? Or vice versa? Why transmute the original film into this medium instead of making a new film…?

Janis:
Before shooting began, Spike invited us to a screening of the original *She's Gotta Have It* from 1986, as well as a documentary about gentrification in Fort Greene where most of the series was shot. Before the screening began, Spike announced "We are not making television, we are making cinema." It was more than a matter of vocabulary, Spike called the episodes "reels," but it went a lot deeper than that.

"Nola does not represent all black women."

Spike directed every episode, seeing each one through the edit with meticulous care and a passion for the very edges of each frame. We watched dailies together as a team every day. Around seven of us—two editors, Hye Mee Na and Randy Wilkens, the DP, Daniel Patterson, producer Elizabeth Hunter, my co-assistant editors David Valdez and Jacqueline Basse, me and Spike—would squeeze into an edit suite at the end of every shooting day and watch 2 to 4 hours of dailies.

It was like being let into Spike's brain in real time as he watched every take of his own creation — it was surreal, educational, and often hilarious. Once the episodes were cut we would watch them weekly in the theater, on the big screen. The way it felt to watch it in a theater, the examination of the frame possible on the big screen, were vital in elevating this from television to cinema. If he could he would make the whole world watch it on the big screen. It makes a difference.

This is the first time Spike has created a series for television. It was Executive Producer Tonya Lewis Lee's idea to base a series on *She's Gotta Have It*. Spike's work spans many genres, so it makes sense that he would foray into the ever- popular world of binge-watching.

In terms of the differences between the mediums, episodic storylines can branch off further from the centerline. More themes can be developed and a wider cast of characters can be explored. Spike took advantage of having more time; his films are almost never shorter than two hours, so having five hours to tell this story was still not enough.

"Give that man a canvas and he will fill it and paint on the back, too."

Katie:

Greer (one of three lovers) says Nola, "has no devotion, allegiance, or loyalty." At the end of the film, we find her happy, alone, scores of candles burning behind her. I think of Ella Fitzgerald singing, "I'm all alone when I lower my lamp. That's why a lady is a tramp." There is something even more subversive about Nola going to sleep alone, rather than with three different lovers. It defies even a need for sexual satisfaction from someone else….

Janis:

I love this ending for the film. As a feminist, it's among my core beliefs that I can have people in my life, but I can also be happy alone. In fact, being happy alone is the prerequisite to having others in my life. I think the "new Nola" reflects this belief, saying "I have to look within to feel what makes me happy."

Into the Vortex: *Vertigo* (1958)
by Lary Wallace[196]

Being a film about obsession, it's only appropriate that *Vertigo* would elicit so much obsession from its admirers, pulling us into the same swirling, inescapable thought patterns that Scottie Ferguson (James Stewart) gets pulled into in his quest to reconstruct a woman he believes to be dead. Just writing that last line makes one realize how ridiculous the premise of *Vertigo* is, but that ridiculousness is part of what gives it its pull, part of how it seduces us into the fever dream of its preposterous premise. It creates a mood unlike that of any other film, and in exploring how that mood was created, one can glimpse a rare and rarefied realm of the filmmaker's art.

The filmmaker of course is Alfred Hitchcock — or at least he's the director. *Vertigo*, somehow, manages simultaneously to both challenge and support the auteur theory, sort of like the camera that zooms and dollys simultaneously to convey Scotty's dizziness as he stares down the abyss of the bell tower. Although you can't imagine *Vertigo* being made by anyone other than Hitchcock, you also can't imagine Hitchcock making it on his own. Too much is reliant on the tone achieved by the score, the primary actors, the set design, the title and animated sequences. *Vertigo* really is, for all this, a supreme example of total film, and the more we stare at it, the more it seems to pull us into its vortex.

Although not even Hitchcock's most fervent admirers would make any claim to the plausibility of his plots, *Vertigo* manages to challenge even these standards of credulity. Many of the film's acolytes have developed a nifty workaround for this, insisting that the whole thing — or the whole thing following Scottie's

---
[196] Lary Wallace is a writer living in Springfield, Missouri.

accident in the beginning — is a dream. That's one way of looking at it, as good as any other, but I prefer instead to embrace the ridiculousness of its scenario, for *Vertigo* is that rare film that transcends such concerns.

But the movie certainly does have a dream-like quality, and it achieves this quality from the very beginning, with designer Saul Bass's hypnotic opening-title sequence.[197] Bernard Herrmann's score — derived from Wagner's *Tristan und Isolde* — plays ominously as a close-up on Kim Novak's face moves from her lower-left quarter to her lips to her upper-right eye. The entire frame becomes red-tinted as the movie's title emerges from her pupil, growing larger and then disappearing. Then, from her pupil comes a spinning spiral, purple and animated. This too becomes large and disappears, before the whole thing gives way to the opening credits, which appear on a black background flanked by another animated spiral. Eventually we're back to the eye, into which the spiral returns. The director's credit emerges from Novak's eye just as the title recently has, and the movie proper begins.

It's hard to know quite what *Vertigo*'s original audience must have made of this eerie, baroque opening. Certainly it signals that something strange is about to occupy the cinema screen — something romantic and psychological, to be sure, but also something murder-mysterious. *Vertigo* is of course all of that. Much later in the film is another animated sequence, this one truly trippy and bizarre, a fever-dream phantasmagoria[198] in which Scottie begins to piece together some of the plot that's been constructed at his expense. Coming two-thirds of the way into the movie, it's an incredibly brazen decision on the part of Hitchcock. To say it's

---

[197] MovieTitleScreens, "Vertigo -- OPENING TITLE SEQUENCE," YouTube (March 22, 2013)
https://www.youtube.com/watch?v=4CZfSc6nJ8U.
[198] Movieclips, "Vertigo (9/11) Movie CLIP - Scottie's Nightmare (1958) HD," YouTube (June 16, 2011)
https://www.youtube.com/watch?v=4WAxDlUOw-w..

unconventional is to say nothing at all. After Scottie dreams this dream, we see him in the very next scene committed to a mental hospital.

The dream sequence wouldn't be half what it is without Herrmann's score. You could say the same about the entire movie, for the way it's able to convey so much interiority, so much of that psychological suspense without which a movie this psychological in nature can simply never come off.

This ability to take the psychological and make it cinematic is a trait shared by all of Hitchcock's collaborators on *Vertigo*. You can start with Kim Novak, the film's leading lady, who played the parts of both Judy and Madeleine, who of course turn out to be the same woman. It's precisely Novak's limitations as an actor, many involved with the film believed, that allowed her to pull off this dual role so cleanly. "If we'd had a brilliant actress who really created two distinctly different people," said Samuel Taylor, one of the film's screenwriters, "it would not have been as good. She seemed so naive in the part, and that was good. She was always believable. There was no 'art' about it, and that's why it worked so very well."

Stewart brought a specialness of his own to a role at least as tricky as Novak's. "I myself had known fear like that," said Stewart, a bomber in World War II, recipient of two Distinguished Crosses, "and I'd known people paralyzed by fear. It's a very powerful thing to be almost engulfed by that kind of fear." You can see it all over his face — the way he's able to convey fright and desperation and jealousy. As his infatuation with Judy builds, so does his frenzy, and by the end, when he at last comes to realize it's all been a setup — that he's fallen in love with a woman who never even existed — he's frantic to the point of insanity. That famous golly-gee voice of Stewart's, normally so endearing, has become wobbly with rage as he interrogates her with his suspicions — now more than suspicions — about her and Gavin Elster: "He made you over, didn't he? He made you over just like I made you over — only better. Not only the clothes and the hair, but the looks and the manner and the words. And those beautiful phony trances!"

This determination of Scottie's to remodel, -fashion, -shape, and -store Judy according to his very own specifications is what makes *Vertigo* such a powerful metaphor for the filmmaker's process, particularly Hitchcock's. And it's this metaphor, in turn, that's done so much to secure Vertigo in the hearts of cineastes as the supreme example of Pure Cinema. "Like James Stewart in *Vertigo*," Donald Spoto writes in his Hitchcock biography *The Dark Side of Genius*, "Hitchcock chose fantasy over reality, and he could not respond to a woman until she was refashioned to correspond with his dream." Spoto keeps it coming, calling Vertigo a "disclosure…of the attraction-repulsion he felt about the object of [his romantic] impulses: the idealized blond he thought he desired but really believed to be a fraud."

What do people mean when they say that San Francisco is a character in *Vertigo*? Just because they apply a facile shorthand doesn't mean they're not talking about something substantial and identifiable. The truth is that the city — its history, its geography, its architecture, even its geology — really does substantively figure throughout the movie: Scottie and Midge go old-bookshop-archival to sniff out the local legend of Carlotta Valdez; the city's famously sloping streets accommodate Scottie's spiraling prowl in search of his fantasy (mysteriously, every turn manages to take him downhill); there is the Golden Gate Bridge where Judy jumps (cantilevered like the bras that Midge designs and that Judy, rather conspicuously, seems to be wearing); there is the redwoods forest and the large, cross-sectioned round of redwood that, where it hangs displaying the geological ages of its rings, resembles nothing so much as a spiral as Scottie and Judy gaze into the enigma of its sphere.

This is the kind of thing Hitchcock was talking about when he said, "The story called for a sophisticated metropolitan setting, and of all those in America, San Francisco fits that — especially in terms of the surrounding country and its architecture."

A fascinating essay could be written on *Vertigo*'s spiral motif alone. I'd read that essay. It would start with the eye — "the first circle," according to Emerson — of Kim Novak that we see in the opening titles, and from there whirl outward to encompass the spirals that represent Scottie's vertigo; the bun in the hair of Judy and Carlotta Valdez; the rings of time in the redwood round; the stairwell Scottie gazes down as Hitchcock's camera, vertiginously, zooms and dollys at the same time. It would loop and lasso all of that and more.

But the most fascinating symbolism to be found in Vertigo is in its color scheme. I don't mind confessing my indebtedness here to a wonderful essay[199] on the YouTube channel Neo. There are plenty of analyses out there on what the colors in *Vertigo* just might mean — what they do mean, in the eye of the beholder — but this is to my mind the most compelling and cogent.

Green represents fantasy — the perversion of reality that occurs when Scottie believes that Judy and Madeleine are two different people, and moreover — paradoxically, impossibly — that they could ever really be the *same* person. It's the color that illuminates Judy (ostensibly from the neon sign outside the hotel room) when she emerges from the bathroom done up for the first time as Madeleine. Even though these two women (Scottie will soon learn) are indeed the same person, they could never, for that very reason, ever be the same to Scottie. You'll recall that Madeleine also, for instance, drives a green car and is surrounded by green in the cemetery to which Scottie follows that green car. When Madeleine is recovering in Scottie's apartment from her

---

[199] Neo, "Vertigo - A Look at Color in Film," YouTube (March 2, 2016) https://www.youtube.com/watch?v=scmHVYYZZ3w.

jump into San Francisco Bay, green is the color Scottie wears as he nurtures her back to wellness. When Scottie sees her for the first time since her presumed death — sees her for the first time as Judy — she is again wearing green.

Blue represents reality. It's the color of the inquest where Scottie is found negligent. It's also the color of the mental hospital where we see him following his breakdown. The color pallette in the hospital is blue not because Scottie is — not because he's depressed, although he's certainly that — but because, consistent with the color's use throughout the film, this is one of those moments when reality is beginning to dawn on him. He's clear-eyed and sober-minded, no longer susceptible to the enchanting fantasies represented by green.

Red represents passion. It's very conspicuously the color of the door to Scottie's apartment where he's caring for Madeleine, and, we're made to understand, falling in love with her. Red is the color of the robe Scottie gives to Madeleine when she awakes from her recuperative slumber. (Her blue dress, like Scottie's sense of reality, has been hung up to dry.)

Yellow is the color we come to associate with Scottie's platonic friend Midge, and, hence, with a kind of comfortable but passionless warmth. Yellow is the color of Midge's apartment walls and of her sweater. Later, when she tries to pique Scottie's passion by painting herself into a portrait of Carlotta Valdez, the sweater she's wearing is red.

One color that Neo's analysis doesn't really address is gray, which, as the color of the suit Madeleine wears early in the film, represents vagueness — the misty cloud of uncertainty. This is the suit Scottie will later make Judy wear to better resemble Madeleine, and as such it's very important to the story Hitchcock wanted to tell. Novak chafed at the idea of wearing the gray suit, believing it a far-from-flattering color for a blond to wear, and registered her protest with fashion designer Edith Head. Head relayed the message to Hitchcock, from whom word came back: *Tell her she can wear any color she wants, as long as it's gray.*

Vertigo is easy to ridicule, if you're not prepared to fall under its oneiric spell, its ambient allure. Orson Welles, for one, could be vicious on the subject — and this was before it replaced *Citizen Kane* as the number-one movie of all time according to the *Sight & Sound* poll. That happened in 2012, and it's always struck me as simple fatigue — among the filmmakers and critics who comprise the poll's voters — with the idea of *Citizen Kane* as the undisputed greatest. It was an expression of the urge for something new. But *Citizen Kane* had held its position for so many years for a reason. It probably really is the greatest film ever made, for those who even believe in such a concept, and whether it's fashionable to say so anymore or not. But if you're willing to nestle down deep into *Vertigo*, indulging its implausibilities, submitting to its silliness, there are plenty of rewards to be found in this sui generis masterpiece in which every element seems to have been refined to its purest embodiment.

One thing about *Vertigo* that doesn't get mentioned nearly enough (if I've seen it mentioned at all, I've forgotten where) is the way the character of Scottie brings something totally new to the identity of the private investigator. Even all these years later, it strikes one as entirely fresh. He doesn't possess the switchblade cool of the Bogie archetype, the uniformly aloof and imperturbable figure from out of film noir. He's vulnerable, and, moreover, he can't help but make his vulnerability show. He's also kind of goofy, particularly when speaking in full-Stewart mode. Let's not forget that he's also the dupe, all the way up until he's not, but by then he's a man undone, no better off for his newly earned knowledge. He's wiser, though — he's got that — and as he stands on the rooftop where Judy has at last fallen to her death — her real death this time — he's someone who's conquered his fears. Cured of his vertigo at last, he's allowed to become a new kind of existential

235

detective-hero, pursuant of a mystery that's psychological rather than criminal in nature, and is therefore never really solved.

Credits

"Could Alex Garland Be Reshaping The Landscape For Female Representation in Science Fiction?," first published at *Medium*, February 1, 2019. Copyright © 2019 Haaniyah Angus.

"How 'The Truman Show' Warned Us About Social Media (Before It Was Invented)," first published at Medium, November 21, 2018. Copyright © 2018 Tom Trott.

"There Is No Spoon," first published at Medium, March 21, 2019. Copyright © 2019 Eric Pierce.

"Screaming Women in Hollywood Horror and Twin Peaks," first published at *Best Damn Writing Magazine*, July 7, 2020. Copyright © 2020 Ariana DiValentino.

"Coraline and Freud. Distinguishing Being and Semblance," first published at Epoch Magazine, December 20, 2017. Copyright © 2017 Timofei Gerber.

"Touch of Evil - 1958," first published at *Moving Image Source* on March 16, 2012; republished at orsonwelles.co.uk. Copyright 2012 © Julien Allen.

"Get Out and The Revolutionary Act of Subverting The White Gaze," First published at *Medium*. Copyright © 2017 Dianca London Potts.

"How Documentary Film Became Entertainment," first published at *Medium*. Copyright 2018 © Joshua Rose.

"This Magnificent Cake Critique," first published at *Best Damn Writing Magazine*. Copyright © 2020 Jumko Ogata.

"Break Up the Media Giants," first published at OneZero/Medium. Copyright © 2019 Paris Marx.

"TCM Diary: Jane Fonda in the 1960s," first published at Film Comment. Copyright © 2020 Beatrice Loayza.

"All Steadicam and No Play: Movement in The Shining," first published at Crooked Marquee. Copyright © 2020 Anya Stanley.

"Black Panther" raises big questions about identity & loyalty," first published at Medium. Copyright © 2018 Doc Ayomide.

"The Beautiful Girls: The Dynamic Women of *Mad Men*," first published at Reel Honey. Copyright © 2019 Angela Morrison.

"Everything Daniel Kaluuya Revealed on The Set of *Queen & Slim*," first published at BET. Copyright © 2019 Jerry Barrow.

"Interpreting the ending of *Crouching Tiger Hidden Dragon*," first published at Medium. Copyright © 2019 Stephen Cobbe.

"*Waves* An Anti-Black Coming of Age Film," first published at Medium. Copyright © 2020 Fatima Ali Omar.

"Miyazaki's Beautiful Antiwar Dreams," first published at Medium. Copyright © 2015 Dan Sanchez.

"Going to The Beginning – The Art of Screenwriting: 1910s," first published at Medium. Copyright © 2020 Seraphima Bogomolova.

"How the Symmetry and Aesthetics of *The Handmaid's Tale* is Essential to Its Storytelling," first published at Film Daze. Copyright © 2019 Zofia Wijaszka.

"The Brilliance of Zack Snyder's DC Universe," first published at Medium. Copyright © 2018 Christopher Pierznik.

"Why Ava DuVernay's *When They See Us* Is The Torturous Masterclass In Systemic Assault," first published at Medium. Copyright © 2019 Ezinne Ukoha.

"'Stay away from the door!': The Women of John Carpenter's *The Fog*," first published at Screen Queens. Copyright © 2019 Sydney Urbanek.

"'We Are Too Rare': The Importance of Inclusivity Behind Spike Lee's *She's Gotta Have It* Reboot," first published at Medium. Copyright © 2017 Katie Tandy.

"Into the Vortex: *Vertigo* (1958)," first published at Medium. Copyright © 2019 Larry Wallace.

Acknowledgments

The Editors, Amir Said and Amir Ali Said:

We would like to thank all of the writers whose work appears in *Samir Cinema, Vol. 1* — Thank you: Haaniyah Angus, Tom Trott, Eric Pierce, Ariana DiValentino, Timofei Gerber, Julien Allen, Dianca London Potts, Joshua Rose, Jumko Ogata, Paris Marx, Beatrice Loayza, Anya Stanley, Doc Ayomide, Angela Morrison, Jerry Barrow, Stephen Cobbe, Fatima Ali Omar, Dan Sanchez, Seraphima Bogomolova, Zofia Wijaszka, Christopher Pierznik, Ezinne Ukoha, Sydney Urbanek, Katie Tandy, and Lary Wallace.

Amir Ali Said acknowledges:

Thank you to my father, Amir Said, for presenting me with this challenge and for offering his guidance and continued advice.
—Amir Ali Said

Amir Said (Said) acknowledges:

Amir Ali Said, my son, best friend, and Superchamp Books co-founder, As always, thank you for your friendship, knowledge, courage, and curiosity. You ran point on this, like I knew you could (would). As always, it was a privilege for me to watch you learn and grow (rapidly) as you assumed the challenge of taking the lead with our first film book anthology. Also, an extra thanks for facilitating so many different tasks in the final hour, I love you, Son, Alhumdulillah!

This book took a lot of careful planning and required the support in various forms from a number of different people (I thank you all!), but there are some people I am compelled to single out here: Géraldine, Thank you for trippling up et Je te remercie — quand on a ajouté le jeudi, c'était plus productif, mais bon, le mercredi est bien gardé, mais plus que ça, merci beaucoup la purée normale;). Christophe, merci pour ta patience et ta compréhension, méme si mon agenda chaque semaine est tres fou. Sibel, thank you for staying on top of things and making sure that I had what I needed, getting to this point would not have been possible without your support; grace à toi, on est bien passé à nouvelle phase — *On n'est pas bien là!* Danni, merci frère, j'espere que l'on va écrire ton livre — thank you for the kind words and the reenforcement for what it means to be Black and living in France; Abdulai, thank you for making everything add up and for always reminding me what must be done next.

—Said

About the Editor

Amir Ali Said is the co-founder of Superchamp Books and the editor of *Samir Cinema*. He is a writer, publisher, actor, and filmmaker from Brooklyn, New York, and a graduate of École Internationale de Création Audiovisuelle et de Réalisation (EICAR - École de Cinéma), Paris, France. His first book, *Performance Day*, was published in 2013. His latest book, *Everyday Routine*, was published in 2017. Amir is the editor of the *Best Damn Hip Hop Writing* series.

About the Series Editor & Creator

Amir Said (*Said*) is the co-founder of Superchamp Books and the creator and series editor of *Samir Cinema*. He is a writer, musician, and publisher from Brooklyn, New York, now living in Paris, France. He has written a number of books including *The BeatTips Manual*, *Ghetto Brother* (co-written with Benjy Melendez), *Medium Speed in the City Called Paris (Poetry)*, and *The Truth About New York*. His new book, *The Art of Sampling, 3rd Edition* will be published in the spring of 2021.

Said is the creator and editor-in-chief of *Best Damn Writing magazine*, the creator and series editor of the *Best Damn Writing book* anthology series, the creator and editor of the *Dating & Sex: Theory of Mutual Self-Destruction* book anthology, and the creator and editor of the *Black Demographic: Essays In Black Life* book anthology.

www.ingramcontent.com/pod-product-compliance
Lightning Source LLC
Chambersburg PA
CBHW070121110526
44587CB00017BA/2878